MINDFUL
LONDON

Tessa Watt is a mindfulness teacher and consultant, running public courses and workshops in organisations since 2009. She is author of *Introducing Mindfulness: A Practical Guide* (2012). In her earlier career she was a research fellow in History at Cambridge University, and a senior producer with BBC Radio and Music. Tessa also teaches meditation at the London Shambhala Meditation Centre, and is a qualified yoga teacher.

MINDFUL
LONDON

How to find calm and contentment
in the chaos of the city

TESSA WATT

CONTENTS

INTRODUCTION

MINDFUL LONDON?

Mindfulness is a simple idea. It means being in the present moment – right here, right now, without wanting it to be somehow different.

That can be a challenge in a big city like London. We Londoners can spend a lot of time thinking about being somewhere else. The giant advertisements in the Underground promise us green fields or a beach with turquoise waters. The sign on the platform says 3 minutes to the next train – but we don't want to be here for the next 3 minutes; we want to be instantly at our destination at the other end of the line, or perhaps even further away on that exotic beach.

Why would we want to be more present? When we look honestly at our minds, we see that much of the time we are somewhere in the past or future, perhaps worrying about our to-do list or replaying an old scenario. Of course there is a place for making plans and for reflection, but much of this mental chatter is repetitive, unproductive and exhausting. When we train our minds to return to the present, we can enjoy life as it is happening. We appreciate all the little moments that we've been missing. We can let go of the spirals of negative thinking which take us into anxiety or depression. Research has consistently shown that mindfulness helps to reduce stress and to increase resilience and wellbeing.

In a big city our resilience can feel constantly challenged. London is a chaotic, noisy, energetic, exciting metropolis. At its best, it exhilarates and inspires us. On a bad day, we feel irritated and agitated by the frenetic pace and the crowds, and by the sheer effort of getting from A to B in one piece.

We may think that mindfulness is all about the opposite – about peace and quiet, stillness and space. So, is 'mindful London' a contradiction in terms?

It's true that most of the core mindfulness techniques involve paring everything down to something simple, like the movement of our breath. We may associate mindfulness with taking a break and getting away from the busyness and distractions of urban life. This is certainly an important part of mindfulness, but it is not the whole story.

This book will embody two sides to mindfulness. On the one hand, we need to take time out to nourish ourselves – to simplify things, stop rushing around and make time for 'being' rather than 'doing'. This guide will include suggestions for places and ways you can do this: quiet gardens and cafés, open spaces, peaceful spots for reflection and exercises to nourish body and mind.

But the ultimate aim of taking time out is to be able to leap back in – to be more present, awake and aware within our normal daily life. The real aim is to appreciate all the little details that make up our lives, and our city. When we walk from the Tube station to work, can we look up and notice the architecture on the street, or hear the birds, or watch the faces of the passers-by? Can we let our environment wake us up out of autopilot so we can enjoy our lives instead of rushing through them?

Mindfulness practice uses simple techniques for training the mind which have traditionally been called 'meditation', but in this approach they are not linked to any religion or belief system. The old stereotype depicted meditators as sandal-clad hippies, but these days a more accurate image would be suited professionals meditating while sitting on chairs in an office meeting room. Mindfulness is taught to staff in leading corporations and institutions like Parliament and the Home Office. Selfridges department store recently created a silent room in which its shoppers can 'celebrate the power of quiet'. Interestingly, this concept was part of the original store a century earlier: in 1909 Henry Gordon Selfridge created a Silence Room where busy shoppers could 'retire from the whirl of bargains and the build up of energy'. Those Edwardian Londoners could also rely on age-old traditions like the Sunday 'day of rest' to balance the demands of work and city life. With these traditions gone, we might all start to ask ourselves how we can re-integrate this natural human need for periods of silence and stillness into the fabric of our modern city. How could we create a more mindful London for the millions who share this vast, ever-changing metropolis?

A MINDFUL JOURNEY PLANNER

If you've picked up *Mindful London* with no experience of mindfulness, you are very welcome. You might like to start with Chapter I to find out a bit more about the history and practice of mindfulness. You'll also find some simple exercises to get you started.

If you already have a sense of what mindfulness is about, feel free to dive in anywhere. Each chapter is organised around a theme: nature, commuting and travelling, art and architecture, silence and solitude, sounds and music, food and drink, movement and learning mindfulness. You'll find suggestions for specific places where you can go to enjoy being mindful in an environment that is restful, spacious or inspiring. You'll also find ideas to help you notice and appreciate more around you when you go on your everyday travels throughout the city. There are practical mindfulness exercises you can try out in the park, on the bus or in a café. By integrating moments of mindful presence into your day, you can discover for yourself how to bring a greater sense of calm into the midst of chaos. You won't stop urban living being busy, but you can find contentment within that busyness, and enjoy the simple experiences that make life worth living.

If you'd like to follow in sequence, this journey starts in Chapter 2 with London's wildlife. For many of us, Nature is our most natural teacher of mindfulness. Trees are naturally mindful; they remind us of a different sense of time and pace. The Woodland Trust even has a hunt for the most ancient trees: the huge, fat, gnarled ones that inspire a sense of mystery and awe. We'll go on a pilgrimage to locate the ancient trees of London, and we'll also find out what species you're most likely to see on your ordinary daily travels; not so that you can become wildlife experts, but to help you see what's around you with fresh eyes.

London is a city veined with green – wherever you are, chances are you are close to a garden, square, park or common. We'll seek out these hidden green spaces, as well as watery places – ponds, canals and the River Thames, the slow artery of the city. We'll also keep our eyes out for the non-human denizens of the city – the birds, cats and foxes who can stop us in our tracks and wake us up to a bigger, stranger world beyond our worries about tonight's dinner or tomorrow's deadline.

Travelling is the thing that Londoners complain about most. London is a big city, and it feels like we spend half our lives trying to make our way from one side of it to the other. We get trapped in crowds, frustrated by delays beyond our control. How can we turn those minutes and hours of travelling time into something more nourishing, less depleting? Chapter 3 will suggest some ways of enjoying the journey, including mindfulness exercises you can practise on the bus, Tube or train.

As well as nature, London's man-made environment can lift us out of our mental fog to help us reconnect with a sense of beauty and inspiration. London is a great cultural capital, but we may forget to enjoy it. Many of us visit the galleries for the big must-see shows, exhausting ourselves as we read every caption and tick off every picture. Chapter 4 introduces the approach of the Slow Art movement. Instead of rushing through an exhibition, spend a long time with one picture. Ten minutes, twenty minutes – really looking. *Mindful London* will suggest a few of the smaller galleries conducive to this more restful pace, or if you're passing by the National Gallery or Tate Modern, step in for a few minutes and look at just one artwork.

*

The city itself is a great outdoor art gallery, with its architecture from several centuries, embodying the creativity of countless Londoners in decorating their built environment, as well as architects and artists from around the globe. London is a city of many influences, from different cultures and times, which is part of what makes it such an exciting place to live in and visit. It's easy to rush along with our eyes fixed downwards onto the pavement, and our head in the next thing we have to do, missing the intriguing details of our streetscapes. Recently I've been noticing more the little decorative elements on the houses and shops I pass on my travels – Victorian turrets, mock-Tudor chimneys, Edwardian stained-glass windows. I'll suggest a few things to look out for – again, not with the aim of becoming architectural boffins, but to help us to be more aware of the world and encourage us to look more fully at our surroundings. Instead of sleepwalking along in a daze, we can let the environment wake us up, noticing the shapes and colours and textures. Enjoying the richness of the cityscape helps us to let go of our worries and enjoy the freshness of a bigger world.

In order to nurture our ability to be mindful as we go about our busy day, we also need moments when we can get away from the crowds and take refuge in silence and stillness. Chapter 5 will explore indoor spaces, including churches and other inspiring buildings, where we can refresh our spirits in the midst of a hectic day. We'll also look at bookshops and libraries where you can nurture the quiet pleasures of reading and browsing, and at a few

London spas where you might consider giving yourself a whole day or evening out, now and then, to let your mind and body rest deeply and be nurtured.

Silence is wonderful, in its place, but the cacophony of the city is also something we can learn to appreciate. Chapter 6 will invite you to try listening to the sounds we normally find irritating and hear them in a different way: sirens, airplanes and car alarms can become an urban symphony if we let them. London is also a city full of music; there is background music everywhere, and that has its place, creating an atmosphere at a pub, café or bar. But in *Mindful London* we'll focus on music for listening – really listening. I'll suggest a few venues with wonderful acoustics, designed for hearing every note, whatever style of music you're into. I'll also suggest some festivals and events that you can count on to provide a feast of classical, jazz, folk, experimental or popular music, where you can give over your whole being to the act of listening.

Chapter 7 will focus on mindful eating and drinking. Any kind of tasting can be mindful: simply paying attention to the food, instead of multi-tasking and getting to the last bite without really tasting it. However, when we eat mindfully we may find we appreciate good quality. We might become more mindful about where our food comes from and how it is produced. This is the rationale behind the 'slow food' movement, and London's many farmers' markets which showcase local produce. The same goes for drinking: we'll look out for some London beers, and places where you can enjoy a drink with the aim of savouring each mouthful rather than knocking it back.

After eating well, we all know we need to get exercise, but this often seems to be a battlefield: a matter of forcing the body into the gym, and overriding any pain or tiredness with our steely will. Chapter 8 will explore the idea of 'mindful movement': learning to pay attention to our body sensations so that we exercise in a way that is led by the body, rather than the mind's idea of what the body should be doing. While any kind of movement can be mindful, slower practices such as yoga and tai chi can be helpful in giving us time to focus on what the body is telling us. Another very accessible form of mindful movement is swimming, giving us the chance to synchronise body and mind in the flow of limbs through water. We'll also look at opportunities to join the new movement for mindful running, casting off the iPod and using the act of running as a chance to be fully present instead of escaping into our own world.

Chapter 9 offers guidance on how you can develop and deepen your experience of mindfulness by taking a course or joining drop-in sessions at a meditation centre. While mindfulness practices do encourage us to enjoy being alone with ourselves, it's also helpful to practise with other people and share your experience of the techniques. You can even join meditation flash mobs that gather together in outdoor locations around the city, from Trafalgar Square to Covent Garden. Sitting in meditation posture might once have been part of the hippy fringe, but now thousands of meditators of all ages and backgrounds are practising in many settings around the city, from corporate offices to public squares.

YOUR MINDFUL CITY

Each week I teach mindfulness classes to groups of Londoners from all walks of life. They share their challenges in finding time for mindfulness practices within hectic urban lives, often squeezed by unworkable hours and the demands of big-city living. But they also share moments of revelation as they find ways to bring a mindful approach into this busyness. Not only in making time for the formal mindfulness practices, but also finding their own moments of space and calm. A few minutes of mindful breathing on the bus or train; a walk through Regent's Park on the way to work; stopping their bicycle on Battersea Bridge to watch the sunset; a moment's pause at the doorstep to appreciate a tree in blossom; slowly sipping a coffee and watching the passers-by.

As well as sharing my own discoveries, this book will draw on the experience of these many Londoners – teachers, accountants, doctors, actors, designers, parents, students – and their insights into living a mindful life. The Guide section of each chapter will offer a few examples of places that I and others have found conducive to mindful experience, but these are not remotely intended as a definitive list: they are suggestions which I hope will spark you to discover and rediscover your own favourite spots where you can take a breathing space or enjoy nature, art, music, food and movement. The practical exercises throughout the book will, I hope, trigger your own ideas about how you could bring greater awareness and appreciation into your everyday activities. *Mindful London* is an invitation to wake up more fully to your own London – whether you're a resident or visitor – and to notice the little experiences that make up daily life in one of the world's great cities.

MINDFULNESS
THE BASICS

If your mind was a city, which city would it be? Would it be laid out in a neat grid like Manhattan or Toronto? Elegant and airy like Paris? A simple village with green fields? Or chaotic, noisy, eccentric, unpredictable, crowded – by turns inspiring and infuriating. Like London?

London is an impossible city. Look at it from above, say from the top of the London Eye, and it makes no sense. A mish-mash of buildings from every period, a wiggly, curving river, randomly angled streets, no easy way to tell 'north' from 'south'.

Mindfulness starts from recognising that our minds are a bit like this hectic crazy city. Our minds are surprisingly random, and very full. Full of worries, stories, images, clever ideas, half-finished conversations, shopping lists, fantasies and fears. The thoughts get clogged up like traffic at a roundabout, or double-decker buses coming along all at once. We might feel sometimes that we would like to clear them all away, and get back to the thatched village with the green fields.

So will mindfulness provide us with this sense of calm and simplicity? The answer is both yes and no. Yes, mindfulness can help us to slow down, relax, and reconnect with the simple experience of being alive, but not by bulldozing everything away. Rather, we can just stop, right here, right in the middle of the busyness, and breathe, and notice. We can sit down for a moment on a bench – real or metaphorical – and for a few moments watch the world go by. If we do it often enough we will create a sense of space within the chaos, and be able to take delight in the creative energy of the city – the big city outside and the internal city of our own minds.

Try this: take a pause

Take a few seconds' break from your reading to notice whatever is here, in yourself and your environment. How does your body feel – are you tired or energised, tense or relaxed, buzzy or lethargic? Are there any thoughts whirling about, or emotions? Notice the space around you – the sights, sounds or smells. See if you can open up your awareness to whatever is here, without judging or analysing what you find.

Now take a few mindful breaths: being aware of the movement of the breath in and out of your body. You don't have to change your breathing, let it be as it is. Notice the breath wherever you feel it, perhaps in the nostrils, throat, chest or belly.

Then carry on. Without making a big deal of it, continue with your day. Each time you find yourself stuck in fast-forward mode, press the pause button and take a few moments out. If you do this often, it will start to puncture holes in your busyness and create a greater sense of spaciousness in your daily life.

The practice of pausing is not a substitute for more formal mindfulness practice – the two go hand in hand. When we 'practise' mindfulness we make time to step out of our normal whirlwind of activity and cultivate our ability to be present; to connect with a greater sense of spaciousness. Then, as we begin to train our minds, we can also let this permeate our daily lives through small and frequent pauses throughout the day. When we become trapped in the claustrophobia of busy thoughts, we can open up to a bigger space – rather like creating gaps in a dense cloud so that the sun can shine through.

WHAT IS MINDFULNESS?

It sounds very simple: paying attention, in this moment; being awake and aware. This is a basic human skill, there is nothing mystical or complicated about it. Yet for some reason we find this so difficult to do. If we look closely at our own minds, we will probably see that we spend a lot of time in a mental fog. London used to be renowned for the thick, heavy fogs that enveloped the city, created by the smoke from millions of chimneys. Now, our air is much clearer, but still we may find ourselves walking around in a fog of our own devising, hardly noticing what is here in front of our noses. We go into 'autopilot' mode, eating our breakfast without tasting it, walking to the Tube without noticing the sky or the buildings or our fellow Londoners as we go on our way.

The problem with being on autopilot is that it takes us into well-worn grooves in our mind, which are often negative ones. A small event can trigger a train of rumination which ends up in irritation, anxiety or depression. Maybe our friend doesn't return a text and it sets us off – almost without us noticing – into thinking that they don't care about us, and they never cared about us, and no one cares about us. Before we know it we're in a black mood, without knowing how we got there. Or maybe there's a delay on the Underground and within a few minutes this inconvenience has turned into a drama about how our whole life is miserable and worthless. Mindfulness gives us a way to recognise when we get stuck on autopilot, and to step out into the freshness of the present moment. Then, we can appreciate the richness of the world and all the little experiences that make up our everyday life.

Luckily, this ability to be present is something that people over the centuries have discovered can be trained – a bit like strengthening a muscle. So we have mindfulness techniques in which we deliberately practise bringing our attention back, again and again, to a particular focus which is here in our present experience – for example the breath, the body, sounds, the environment. I will also refer to meditation in this book. However, it's good to be aware that some forms of meditation have somewhat different purposes from those we are exploring here, such as cultivating altered states of consciousness, or connecting with the divine. In this book we are talking about meditation as a simple and basic act of training the mind to be more present and aware.

In addition to formal meditation practice, we can also bring mindfulness more informally into the activities of daily life, such as walking, brushing our teeth, making a cup of tea, or simply pausing to notice what is here. When we wash the dishes, instead of resenting every minute of it, we can enjoy the warm soapy water, the shine of the plates, the satisfaction of getting the dishes clean. At any moment we can drop our mental chatter and discover appreciation for simple experiences, bringing wakefulness and a greater sense of contentment into our lives.

BRINGING AWARENESS TO THE BREATH

The breath is probably the oldest and most common focus for mindfulness. When you feel your breath you are connecting with the basic feeling of being alive. In every moment you are breathing, most of the time without noticing, so it's a natural tool for bringing yourself back to the present moment. When you tune in to your breathing, your body and mind are in synch: the breath is a bridge between the two. Whenever you get caught up in a maelstrom of thoughts, you can let them go and come back to the cool breeze of the breath. The more you become familiar with the breath, the more it becomes a haven for your awareness – something you can trust. Here you are, with this breath, now.

Try this: mindfulness of breath

This simple mindfulness practice can be done for any length of time – five minutes is a good start. You can build up to 10, 20 or 30 minutes, or do a shorter practice of two or three minutes. Choose a quiet place to do this while you're getting used to the technique, but after that you can practise anywhere – on the train, at your desk, in a waiting room.

- **Take a good posture**: Sit on a chair with your feet flat on the floor, or sit cross-legged on a firm cushion. Let your spine be tall, your shoulders relaxed, and your hands resting naturally on your thighs; placing your palms facing down can help to keep you grounded. Close your eyes, or keep them open with a downward gaze, whichever is most comfortable. Your posture can be relaxed but wakeful.

- **Grounding**: Feel the weight of your body, the sense of gravity. Bring your attention to the sensations of your feet in contact with the floor, and your bottom on the seat. Spend a few moments exploring these feelings of contact with the ground which is supporting you.

- **Breathing**: Notice the fact that you are breathing. You don't have to change the breath in any way, just let it be as it is. Bring your awareness right up close to the physical sensations of the breath, wherever you feel it. Is it in the nostrils, or the back of the throat, or the chest, or the belly, or some combination of these places? Can you feel the texture of it, the length of it? See if you can *be with* the breath, rather than *thinking about* the breath. Allow the breath to breathe itself, and just ride the waves – all the way in, and all the way out.

+ **Coming back**: Each time you notice your mind has wandered off, gently return your attention to the breath. You'll probably find you have to do this over and over again – that 's completely normal. Perhaps within seconds you're no longer here, you're replaying a scene from work, or daydreaming, or planning tonight's dinner. Just notice you've been gone, and gently escort your awareness back to the breath. This is the practice of mindfulness: not expecting to keep the mind perfectly focused, but being willing to let go of whatever took you away, and come back, over and over.

As you become familiar with this practice, the breath will slowly become available to you in any moment, as an anchor to bring you back to the here and now. The practice is simple, but powerful. It may seem like you spend the whole time thinking, and that nothing of benefit is happening, but try to do it without expectation of immediate benefits, because the practice takes time to work, and can seep into your being at an almost cellular level. Each time you do this practice, you are strengthening your mindfulness muscle in a way that can start to have an impact on the rest of your life.

A history of mindfulness in five breaths

A deep breath: Mindfulness has been practised for thousands of years. Many cultures have taught ways to let go of mental chatter and be present in this moment as part of their spiritual traditions. Mystics and meditators have emphasised the importance of 'being' as well as 'doing', such as the 12th-century Abbess Hildegard of Bingen, who described herself as 'a feather on the breath of God'. Eastern philosophies such as Buddhism have taken a particular interest in how the human mind works, developing techniques for training focus and presence.

An intake of breath: From the 1960s, Western interest in Eastern meditation was given a big boost by the influx of teachers from Vietnam, India, Japan and Tibet into Europe and America. The Chinese invasion of Tibet may have crushed Buddhist culture in its heartland, but it meant that centuries of insight from this isolated mountain kingdom were now released into the rest of the world, mixing with Japanese Zen and the more body-oriented hatha yoga from India. Meditation and yoga became a big part of the counter-culture, from the Beat poets to The Beatles.

A breath of fresh air: In 1979, an American molecular biologist named Jon Kabat-Zinn became interested in how he could bring his experience of yoga and Buddhist meditation into Western medicine. He created an 8-week course at the University of Massachusetts Medical School to help people with difficult conditions such as chronic pain, AIDS and cancer to relate to their stress and suffering in a different way. The success of Kabat-Zinn's 'Mindfulness-based Stress Reduction' (MBSR) brought meditation out of the hippy fringe and into the mainstream of medicine and science.

An out-breath: MBSR began to spread around the globe, not only for people with illnesses, but for thousands wanting to increase their general wellbeing and enjoy life more fully. The structured, secular format made it accessible to people from all backgrounds, especially those who might have been put off by any religious trappings. In the 1990s, a group of clinical psychologists from the UK and Canada developed Mindfulness-based Cognitive Therapy (MBCT) – similar to MBSR with a bit more emphasis on how to work with negative thinking which can lead to depression. There's been an explosion of public courses, and the mindfulness movement is spreading in business and other workplaces, including a cross-party mindfulness course in the Houses of Parliament. The Mindfulness in Schools Project has developed a special programme for teenagers, helping students to think more clearly and be less reactive to stress.

A shallow breath? Mindfulness is becoming a buzzword, with a flow of books (even *Mindful London*!), media coverage, and marketing – a friend recently gave me a chocolate bar with 'Mindfulness Matters' on the wrapper. All good? I think mainly, but like anything, when ideas become popular their essence can get diluted. Mindfulness gets jumbled together with positive psychology, dieting, hypnotherapy and other kinds of therapies – all perhaps good things in their own right, but each has their own different aims and emphases. Mindfulness is simple, but also profound, and can unlock a radically different way of being in the world. If you become seriously interested in where this practice might lead you, visit Chapter 9 for some suggestions on how to connect with people in London who practise mindfulness as a lifelong journey, on which there is always more to discover.

THE BODY

Mindfulness sounds like it's all about the mind, but it's just as much about the body – about being *embodied*. While the mind goes flitting off on its travels, the body is always here, where we are right now. When we bring our mind into the body, we are present – it anchors us. Fully inhabiting our body we feel healthy, grounded and stable, and from this place we can cope with life's challenges.

When we listen to the body we also find it has a lot to tell us. It is constantly registering our experience, tensing and bracing against the things we find difficult, relaxing and softening with experiences we find enjoyable. Imagine a scenario: perhaps you're late for a meeting, stuck on a hot crowded train, and the driver announces a delay. What happens in your body at this moment? Does your stomach clench, or your shoulders tighten? When irritations and emotions come there is a kind of raw energy in the body which we may find uncomfortable, and we try to get rid of it by shouting and stomping, or we clench up and try to block them out. Mindfulness trains us to be able to notice body sensations – whether pleasant or challenging – and just let them be without having to react to them. Paying attention to the body we find we are able to experience and handle the flow of our life as it happens, rather than over-reacting or pushing down our difficult feelings, which then find ways of making themselves known in the form of anxiety, stress or depression.

Mindfulness courses often begin with a practice called the 'body scan', a technique in which you bring awareness to different parts of the body in turn. This is usually done lying down, with a teacher's voice to guide you. The full practice isn't so easy to follow from a book, but you can find audio downloads on the web (see resource list). Here's a shorter version of the body scan which you can do sitting in a chair – or even on the bus or train – to give you a flavour.

Try this: a short sitting body scan

The purpose of this practice is not to achieve any special goal, but to be with whatever is here in this moment, as best you can, without judgement. Notice when you go off into *thinking about* your experience, and see if you can come back to your direct experience, through the senses. The body scan helps us to move from thinking about the body to feeling it from the inside: to being fully embodied.

* **Settling in**: Take a good posture, feeling the weight of your body; notice the sensations of contact with the floor and the seat. Feel the movement of the breath in your body. You could place a hand or hands on your belly, and bring awareness to the sensations in your abdomen, expanding and falling back gently like a balloon.

* **Feeling your toes**: Bring your awareness down into your left toes, noticing any sensations here. Can you feel contact with the sock or shoe – a tingling, warmth or cold, or no sensations at all, just a blank? There's no correct thing to feel, just spend a few moments noticing whatever is here. Now imagine you can breathe all the way down your body into your left toes, and then back up from the toes, out through the nose or mouth. Don't worry if it doesn't make complete sense, but try playing with this for a few breaths – breathing down into the toes, and back out from

the toes. You might have a feeling of your breath and awareness moving together.

• **Feet and legs**: Let go of your focus on the toes, and broaden your attention to the whole of the left foot. Notice any sensations of contact, heaviness, tightness, softness, aching – whatever is here. Continue the same process as you slowly move your awareness up through the left leg – from the ankle up the calf and shin, knee and thigh – noticing the sensations. Broaden your awareness to take in the whole of the left leg. Now see if you can have a sense of breathing into the whole of the leg, filling it with breath. On an out breath, let go of your focus on the left leg and continue the same process with the right leg, starting with the right toes, right foot, and moving up the leg.

• **Rest of the body**: Move your awareness up through the body. Notice your buttocks on the seat, your hips and pelvis, torso, arms and hands, shoulders, neck and head. You can spend as much time as you like in each place, or scan through fairly quickly. Notice sensations in each region, without judgement. If you find any sensations that are difficult, see if you can be gently curious about them, rather than blocking them out or struggling with them. If there's tension or pain, is it sharp or dull, constant or changing, does it have a shape and a texture? Play with 'breathing into' each part of the body before you move away, sensing the breath flowing into and out from that area.

• **Coming back**: Don't worry if your mind wanders off, this is natural. Each time you notice your attention has strayed into thoughts, gently escort it back to the body.

- **Resting**: At the end, spend a few moments resting, with a sense of the whole body sitting here, and with awareness of the movement of the breath.

The body scan gives us a chance to re-inhabit the body and feel its natural qualities of groundedness and stability. Even if we have difficult sensations, we find that we can handle them, letting them be as they are. We discover the body as a place we can trust and come back to.

MAKING FRIENDS WITH YOUR MIND

As you do any mindfulness practice, see if you can cultivate a gentleness and good humour in the way that you bring your mind back to the focus. Are you being hard on yourself for not doing it 'right'? It's common to feel you are rubbish at it, and that you have a uniquely unruly mind – almost all of us think this! This leaping about like a monkey is exactly what the human mind does, and a big part of the practice is making friends with your mind. One of the key attitudes we cultivate in mindfulness practice is 'non-judgement': learning to be more accepting of ourselves, and through this, more accepting of other people and situations.

If we watch how our mind works we may notice that a lot of the time there's a sense that things are not quite how we want them to be, or that we ourselves are not what we should be, or perhaps it is other people who are letting us down. How much less exhausting it would be to drop this struggle with the present moment and accept how things actually are.

You can nurture this attitude in your mindfulness practice, and with time you may find that it percolates into the rest of your life. You might start to see how hard you are on yourself, and develop a sense of kindness and good humour. When you find yourself stressed out or caught up in a whirlwind of thoughts, be gentle – it's not about expecting to be mindful 24 hours a day. We all move in and out of autopilot, including those of us who've been practising mindfulness for years. We all sometimes miss our stop on the Tube, or find ourselves with the key in the door of our flat when we meant to stop at the corner shop to buy bread.

When we notice we're being unmindful or absent-minded, we can have a sense of humour about it. 'Oops, there I go again!' True masters of mindfulness, like the Dalai Lama, seem to chuckle a lot at the humour of daily life. As we nurture a feeling of friendly good humour towards ourselves, this can naturally affect the way we are with others. In a big city like London, it is easy to find ourselves constantly irritated with other people. They get in our way on the pavement – they walk too slowly or too quickly; they push ahead of us in a queue; they crowd up against us in the Tube or bus, invading our personal space. We stop seeing them as humans, so we stop smiling at them and making human contact. But with mindfulness we can reconnect with our natural friendliness towards both ourselves and others.

THE BENEFITS:
THE SCIENCE OF MINDFULNESS

There's been an explosion of research into mindfulness within the last few decades. New studies come out every month demonstrating the benefits of these practices for both physical and mental health. Increasingly, doctors and therapists are recommending mindfulness courses for patients with stress, depression and anxiety. Thousands of people are taking up mindfulness to improve their general wellbeing.

These are some of the benefits that have been identified by research into mindfulness:

◆ **Reducing stress**. When we get over-stressed, our automatic nervous system goes into overdrive – the 'fight or flight' mechanism. Mindfulness practice allows the body to calm down from this state, an effect which has been measured in lower levels of the 'stress hormone' cortisol.

◆ **Reducing rumination**. Several studies have shown that mindfulness reduces rumination, the compulsive, repetitive thinking which can lead to the development of depression. The UK's National Institute for Health and Care Excellence (NICE) recommends mindfulness for patients with a history of recurrent depression.

◆ **Focus, memory and flexibility**. Studies have shown groups of mindfulness meditators performing better than control groups in tasks measuring their ability to focus attention, their working memory and their cognitive flexibility – the ability to integrate information in a new way.

- **Coping with pain and illness.** After a short training in mindfulness, participants reported a higher pain threshold – that is, the same levels of pain which were formerly experienced as distressing had now become more bearable. By practising mindfulness, many patients were found to cope better with chronic pain and with the symptoms of a range of illnesses from arthritis to cancer to multiple sclerosis.

- **Strengthening the immune system.** Mindfulness has been shown to improve the body's response to illnesses ranging from flu to psoriasis to HIV.

- **Increased wellbeing.** Neuroscientists are investigating the idea that meditation can strengthen areas of the brain associated with happiness, wellbeing and compassion. MRI scans have shown that areas of the brain cortex linked to wellbeing and empathy are thicker in people who practise mindfulness. Just as we can strengthen muscles with physical exercise, it seems that mindfulness training can strengthen areas of the brain, with measurable results.

So is mindfulness the great new cure for all evils? The current research does suggest some of the same benefits that meditators themselves have been reporting for years, if not centuries. Many of these studies are showing measurable effects in groups who've been practising for a relatively short time, such as graduates of an 8-week course, so the good news is that you don't have to become a Buddhist monk to experience improved health and wellbeing.

Mindfulness can be challenging, and in some ways it's still counter-cultural. So much of our advertising and media and peer pressure is telling us to speed up, and to fill every moment of our already busy lives with some form of entertainment or *doing*. It can feel like a radical act to stop for even five minutes and do seemingly nothing, or not very much. But many of us know in our bones this is exactly what we need to do in order to ride the energy of urban life – and enjoy it. To put on the brakes; to pause; to create space in little ways wherever we can. This book is an invitation to start that journey, and to explore for yourself what a mindful life could be in the context of 21st-century London.

NATURALLY
MINDFUL

Nature is naturally mindful. The sparrows fluttering in the tree outside my window don't seem to be ruminating on the past or the future, and nor does my cat, stretched out on her back and purring. They are present. When we pay attention to nature it helps us be present too.

We know instinctively that spending time in nature is healthy for mind and body, and now scientific studies are producing the evidence to back this up. In the city, we have to remain constantly vigilant, avoiding obstacles such as cars and screening out an excess of irrelevant stimuli. Research shows that being in natural settings restores our cognitive functions and revives our ability to focus. Nature is filled with inherently interesting stimuli that capture our attention in a more restful, less directed way. As we instinctively stop and notice a sunset or an unusual bird, our attentional circuits refresh themselves. Walking in nature is like a holiday for the brain.

In Japan they have a practice called 'Shinrin-yoku' or 'forest bathing'. The idea is to take in the forest atmosphere through all five senses, allowing your body and mind to unwind. Japanese research has shown that being in nature can significantly lower levels of the stress hormone cortisol, and can also lower blood sugar and decrease blood pressure and heart rate. The biologist Edward O. Wilson coined the term '*biophilia*', which means 'love of life or living systems' to describe our instinctive urge to connect with the vitality of the natural world. I find that at times I get cravings for greenery in the same way that I crave a salad – I could almost eat the leaves off the trees.

Many Londoners satisfy this need to be amongst nature by heading to the countryside at the first opportunity; jumping in cars and clogging up the motorways on Bank Holiday weekends. However, we can strengthen our connection with nature and its healing properties in the course of our daily urban lives. London itself is full of green; from secret garden squares to the vast open spaces like Richmond Park, the woods of Hampstead Heath, the commons of south London and the string of Royal Parks through the city centre. Around every corner lies a little piece of the natural world. Tapping into the refreshing power of nature is not only about seeking out these green spaces but also paying more attention to the flora and fauna as part of your normal routine, noticing the blossom in front gardens on your walk to the Tube station or the squirrels playing in the tree outside your window.

OPEN SPACES

Modern city living can feel claustrophobic: the hassles of dealing with teeming crowds are often mirrored in our mental world, which feels crowded with thoughts, worries and sensory overload. When our minds feel congested like this, it can be wonderful to seek out the experience of open space – literal and physical. Where there's a vista and an open sky, there's a natural sense of perspective – the world is bigger and we're open to possibilities.

There are over a hundred registered commons in London, ranging from small slices of land to large expanses. The eight Royal Parks of London – former royal hunting grounds – cover an astonishing 1,976 hectares. When I asked participants from my mindfulness courses about their favourite mindful places they mentioned their local commons, from Hampstead Heath to Clapham Common – parklands where they can look out over an expanse of green and connect with a sense of space.

Walking the dog, if you have one, is a great excuse to spend mindful time outdoors. It can be a chore that you hurry through, feeling resentful, or it can be a precious chance each day to feel your feet on the ground and enjoy the experience of open space, wind and weather. Walking in general is one of the best ways to spend time in nature, clear our heads and reconnect with our bodies. (See Chapter 3 for an exercise of mindful walking.) Many of us associate serious walking with heading for the Yorkshire Moors or the Cornish coast, but there are a number of beautiful long-distance routes in and around London. You could work your way around these walks – one segment at a time – as a way of discovering unknown commons, canals, forests and fields across the city. (See walklondon.org.uk)

The weather is a constant topic of conversation in London, as everywhere in Britain, where the vagaries of island weather mean we can have bitter wintry cold in the midst of summer, or a mild spring-like day in winter. With a mindful approach we can allow ourselves to feel the rawness of the weather, rain or shine. We might notice if we're bracing ourselves against the cold and drizzle, wasting energy on irritation and resentment. Perhaps we can relax with how things are, taking a moment when we step outside to feel the freshness of rain, the sharpness of cold, the warmth of sun, with some sense of equanimity, enjoying our contact with the elements.

Try this: park bench

Take a few minutes' break on a park bench, stone wall or other outdoor seat.

- Feel your feet flat on the ground, and your bottom on the seat. Your eyes can be open or closed. Notice the contact with the earth and the weight of your body.

- Bring your awareness to your breath, feeling the physical sensations of breathing without needing to change anything. Feel the gentle breeze of breath moving in and out of your body.

- Now broaden your awareness to have a sense of your whole body, and any sensations of the weather that you can feel. Are you warm or cool, damp or dry? Can you feel sunshine, or mist, or the movement of a breeze somewhere on your skin? Notice if you are bracing against the weather in some way, and see if you can relax with how things are in this moment.

- Now open your awareness to other senses. You might like to focus on listening for a few moments, picking up the sounds of birds or children or traffic without bias. (For more on mindful listening, see Chapter 6.) Are there any smells – perhaps the freshness of the wind, or the scents of flowers? If your eyes are closed, you could open them and allow your gaze to take in the visual field, with its rich colours, shapes and textures. When you find yourself drifting off into thoughts, bring yourself back to the feeling of your weight on the seat, or to some other aspect of your sensory experience.

HIDDEN GARDENS

Garden squares are one of the unique features of London – no other city has developed them in quite the same way. The layout of Georgian and Victorian squares created leafy spaces which are a haven for wildlife as well as vital links in the green chain between the city's parks and domestic back gardens. The earliest squares – laid out in the 17th century – were really just open grassed areas, surrounded by wooden fences and gravelled walkways. The first square to have a proper garden at its centre was probably Soho Square, created as a pleasure garden in 1681 by the Earl of Macclesfield, with ornamental flowers, shrubs and trees. Knowing a little of this history helps us appreciate the legacy of past Londoners who enjoyed reflective time in nature and left us these natural mindful spaces in the midst of our urban world.

Many garden squares are private, but public squares like Russell Square, Lincoln's Inn Fields and Soho Square are the perfect place to go for a breathing space. The older squares have dense shrubberies and mature trees which create the right habitat for birds to nest and feed, and are home to butterflies, insects and small mammals. Both these gardens and the bigger parklands in the city are, of course, wonderful places to appreciate flowers; from the fresh daffodils and crocuses of spring to the fulsome summer blooms. Taking time to look closely at the delicate shapes and details of a flower can bring us into the present moment and wake us up to the richness of the natural world.

In all these natural spaces we can slow down the pace of our lives as we go about the city. Here we can practise a few minutes of mindful breathing or walking, and open our eyes and ears. As we enter these green places they encourage us to let go of the claustrophobia of our thoughts and worries, and open up to the vivid world of our senses. This shifts our perspective so we feel more spacious and alive as we continue our day.

TREES AND WOODS

Ancient tree hunt

Trees are a reminder to slow down – in the world of trees, everything happens at a different pace. Year after year, the tree grows slowly from seed to sapling to young tree to old veteran. The seasons change, leaves grow, unfurl and drop, winds blow, rains fall, and the tree stands patiently. While flowers remind us of life's impermanence and fragility, trees connect us with stability, strength and a longer view.

Many of London's trees are living relics of an ancient past: centuries old; huge, fat and gnarled. They are older than most of our buildings, older than the railways and Tube lines. Our ten-minute delays and financial worries mean nothing in their presence. To see them brings us into a different sense of time.

The Woodland Trust has a special project called the Ancient Tree Hunt which is a living database of ancient trees (ancient-tree-hunt. org.uk). Through this the trust encourages the public to find and record these trees as a first step towards caring for them, and so far over 100,000 trees have been recorded across the UK. Tree hugging is definitely encouraged, as a 'hug' is the best way of measuring the girth of a tree. Oaks and sweet chestnuts are likely to be classified 'ancient' when they measure more than three or four 'adult hugs', based on the finger tip to finger tip measurement – roughly 1.5 metres.

London trees

Big ancient trees have a special magic, but we can also notice and enjoy the more common trees that we pass on our everyday travels. London is probably the greenest of the world's big cities; our predecessors left us a city softened by trees, with leafy neighbourhoods and plane-lined streets. In 2003 the tree population of Greater London was estimated at around seven million – almost one tree for every Londoner. About 20 per cent of London's land area is under tree cover, with the majority of trees located in gardens and close to 500,000 in streets across the city. If we cultivate our curiosity and interest a little, we may find we notice what's around us with fresh eyes.

Trees can play a big role in being mindful in London; if we start to notice their shapes, colours and characters and their sheer number around the city. Each time we are aware of a tree, for that moment we can connect with the calm, grounded quality of nature within the freneticism of urban life. One participant in my mindfulness course came up with this way of learning more about the trees: 'A few weeks ago a major storm was forecast that put us in mind of the storm of 1987 that destroyed so many trees on the commons in south-west London. Thinking we might again be about to lose a lot of great trees we had taken for granted, we went onto the local common. We collected leaves then came home and identified them in Roger Phillips' book *Trees in Britain*. There were the oak, the chestnut, and the ash as you might expect, but there were also exotic species we'd never heard of – Black Locust (from the American Mid-West), Himalayan Juniper, Pyrenean Oak, fig, Japanese Maple, Lombardy Poplar ... and many more.

'Now when I am on the common I find that I see the trees not as generic leafy things, but individuals with their own stories. Less often do I cross the common in a daze, my mind full of the day ahead or the day past, because, for a few minutes, I really see what is around me. If you go out onto your local green space, or even walk down your street and notice what's growing there, maybe it will change the way you see your bit of London.'

It is not difficult to learn about trees, but apparently our knowledge of them is decreasing: according to the Wildlife Trust, 68 per cent of people older than 55 can recognise an oak leaf, compared with 39 per cent of 18–24-year-olds – and this is the UK's most common tree. Is this a sign that we are becoming less mindful? The most common tree in London itself is the (aptly named) London Plane, which you can recognise by its camouflage-patterned bark and its brown seed balls in winter, which resemble hanging pom-poms. The tree first appeared in Britain in the 17th century, and is thought to be a hybrid of the Oriental and American planes, possibly imported from Spain. Its papery bark, in shades of olive green and grey, has been described as a 'self-cleaning bark' because it sheds large flakes or scales, discarding pollutants it had absorbed and maintaining the health of the tree. With its compact root system and tolerance for pollution it survives well as a roadside and parkland tree: the London Plane is said to account for over half of all trees planted in the city.

At the simplest level, the more we know about what we are seeing, the more we are likely to see and appreciate. You can use a book to identify the trees, or you can look them up on the web: woodlandtrust.org.uk; woodlands.co.uk; nhm.ac.uk (search for 'urban tree survey'). City Lit, a leading centre for adult learning, offers a course on the Trees of London, with classroom talks and visits to local parks and gardens to identify common species (citylit. ac.uk).

WATER: PONDS, CANALS AND RIVERS

If London is veined with green, it has arteries flowing with water – from the great River Thames and its tributaries to the 100-mile network of canals, to the countless ponds on our commons. Water has a naturally soothing quality. If we seek it out, it calms our frayed nerves and cools our irritations. Flowing water reminds us that life isn't rigid, but fluid – we can go with the flow. Still water reflects the sky and the trees, and connects us with the still qualities of the mind.

London was built where it is because of the River Thames, but many of us have little connection with it in our daily lives. Whether it's a Sunday stroll along its banks, or a brisk walk across a bridge in the midst of a working day, it's always worth taking time out to see and experience the river. The Thames Path walk covers 64 kilometres on both sides of the river from Hampton Court Palace, through the heart of the city, to the East India Docks and the marshes of East London. At the time of the Great Stink of 1858, the Thames was overflowing with sewage, but now it is said to be Europe's cleanest major river. So now you can happily stand on its banks and breathe it in through all the senses.

London's network of 18th- and 19th-century canals have a different quality. Ribbons of quiet water move slowly through a hidden world. The towpaths of the Grand Union Canal, Limehouse Cut or Regent's Canal are made for mindful walking or cycling. They have moments where they burst into public view – such as the boating hub of Little Venice or the markets of Camden Lock – but much of the time they flow past the backsides of houses, offices and pubs, past gasworks and warehouses, through a secret parallel city.

Finally, our local commons and parks are dotted with myriad ponds, alive with water birds – ducks, swans, Canada geese, coots, gulls and herons. My nearest common, Wandsworth, has two interlinked ponds which provide a reedy wonderland for wildlife, with benches on which to sit and watch, or to practise mindful breathing. In the words of the Vietnamese meditation master Thich Nhat Hanh: 'Still water can reflect the sky, the clouds, and so on. When the water

is still, it can reflect things as they are; it does not distort things
... That is why to learn how to breathe in and breathe out mindfully,
we can still ourselves, we can calm ourselves ... So still water is
within you. You see things clearly as they are.'

Try this: water meditation

Water has often been used as a metaphor for the nature of the
mind. Sometimes it feels like a stormy ocean, with thoughts
thrashing about like turbulent waves. At other times it may be
more like a still lake, with ripples on the surface. When the mind
is turbulent, we don't achieve anything by trying to suppress the
waves – this only creates a sense of struggle. Instead, the practice
of mindfulness gives a space in which we can relax with the waves
of the mind and let them do their thing. We may find that these
waves calm and settle of their own accord, and when they don't, we
can learn to ride the turbulence, knowing that beneath the surface
there is depth and stillness.

Next time you are beside a pond, canal or quiet stretch of river,
take a few minutes to immerse yourself – metaphorically – in the
sense of the water. Notice if it is flowing or still, or rippled with
tiny waves. Can you see the movement of wind on its surface? Is it
murky or clear; can you see reflections of trees and sky and light?
Do you have a sense of the deeper water beneath the surface?
Can you connect with that feeling of stillness, coolness and depth?

Open all your senses to the water: looking, hearing the birds,
feeling and smelling the breeze. When your mind goes off
somewhere else, gently reel it back in like a fishing rod. Spend

some time letting the atmosphere of the pond or river permeate you, breathing it in.

Before you leave, take a mental photograph of the scene. When you find yourself in the mayhem of urban life, see if you can reconnect with the mental image of the water. Let it soothe and refresh you, and remind you of the stillness and depth of your own mind, no matter how choppy it may feel on the surface.

LONDON WILDLIFE

London's green spaces are teeming with wildlife – from the swans in Hyde Park to the deer in Richmond Park, to the countless birds in our garden squares. If we take just a moment to notice the wild creatures which share our city, they can pull us out of our rumination over our endless human problems and projects, and back into the here and now. Closest to home, if you have a pet, you probably know already how a few minutes stroking the cat or playing with the dog can be a simple, tactile experience which grounds you in the present. Without making a special trip to the zoo, or even going out of our way, there are animals roaming our streets and gardens which we can look out for and observe when they cross our path, which remind and help us to reconnect with our environment. Even the mice scurrying along the tracks of the London Underground can offer us a sudden shift of perspective to their mouse-eye view of our city.

The fox is one of these common London animals. You may dislike or fear them as a menace, or you may love them for their wild beauty. Either way, the moment you find yourself on a London street looking a fox in the eye can be a moment to wake up to the strangeness and vividness of the world. The fox has been part of our urban landscape since the 1930s, when the expanding suburbs began to encroach on their rural territory. London is teeming with some 10,000 foxes – they are so common that apparently 70 per cent of us can report seeing one within the past week. A fox was even discovered living 72 storeys above ground at the top of our tallest skyscraper, The Shard, having apparently climbed up the stairwell and survived on scraps left by builders. At night foxes can be startling, with blood-curdling screams outside the window. Red foxes have a wide vocal range which spans five octaves, so when you hear their high-pitched whines or throaty barks in the night, you can pause a moment to listen and wonder.

Another London animal which gets a bad press is the grey squirrel, but if you can look freshly at squirrels, they are intriguing and lively creatures. They were introduced from North America in the 19th century and were wrongly thought to be responsible for the decline of the native red squirrel (which was in fact wiped out mainly by habitat loss and pest control). Squirrels are so common that we hardly notice them, but take a moment to watch what they are doing – foraging in trees, scurrying along with their noses to the ground, burying their nuts or digging them up, depending on the season. Each squirrel is estimated to hoard their food in several thousand caches every year, which they can locate again when they need it thanks to a very accurate spatial memory.

London has been famous for its resident cats ever since the legend of Dick Whittington, the Lord Mayor of London in the 14th century, who allegedly made his fortune thanks to the rat-catching abilities of his cat. You can find cats on every street – peering out from windows, slinking through gardens, crouching on walls. There they sit, in a different London from ours: they hear three times better than us, they sleep twice as much, they can see in the dark, and when they want to they can run faster than Usain Bolt. Do you pass them by with your head in your to-do list, or do you stop for a moment to notice these strangers in our midst, each with their own character, and wonder what the city might look like through their eyes?

Urban bird-watching

Twitching has become trendy, and groups of hipsters have reportedly taken to peering through binoculars from the rooftops of Shoreditch bars. The self-styled 'urban birder' David Lindo leads bird-watching sessions in Wormwood Scrubs – the grasslands next to the prison – and at the top of Tower 42 in central London. 'When birding in a city, try to see the world as a bird would see it. Ignore people, see buildings as craggy lumps of rock and imagine that the bush you are looking at is filled with food and on a remote headland.' (theurbanbirder.com)

Wildlife havens like the London Wetlands Centre are magnificent places to find rare and interesting species of bird, but many of us can start by just looking up into the sky above us and appreciating some of our most common birds, such as woodpigeons, sparrows, blue tits and starlings. Birds are as much a treat for the ears as for the eyes (see Chapter 6).

SUSTAINABLE CITY LIVING

Mindfulness starts as a private, individual experience, but inevitably when we become more mindful we notice our impact on the environment around us – we might take a more active interest in how we can respond in our own community to the big issues of climate change and shrinking supplies of cheap energy. The Transition Network helps neighbourhoods develop small-scale local responses to these global challenges. There are Transition groups in almost every London borough (london-transition.org.uk), and you can get involved in events ranging from recycling projects to craft workshops to permaculture. Brixton has launched the 'Brixton pound', which encourages people to spend money locally. Kentish Town and Belsize Park are growing hops to create a local brew. Leytonstone, Ealing and other Transition Town groups have community gardens (farmgarden.org.uk). Getting your own allotment in London is very difficult (some councils have waiting lists more than ten years long!), so these community gardens offer a good opportunity to get your hands dirty and relearn the skills of growing food.

MINDFUL GUIDE

Open spaces and hidden gardens

ISABELLA PLANTATION

This is a magical woodland garden, hidden away within Richmond Park. Its 42 acres are fenced off from the rest of the park, secluded by trees and full of exotic plants that explode in a riot of colour every spring. Visit in late April or May for glades of azaleas, rhododendrons, camellias and magnolias blooming in dazzling shades of pink, purple, red, orange and almost every colour in nature or carpets of daffodils and bluebells for a natural experience that feels close to hallucinogenic.

While the plantation is at its most spectacular in spring, it is still interesting year round, with winter flowers, a heather garden and trees with bark of distinctive colours and textures. There are water-lily ponds and a lovely stream bordered with irises and ferns. The Isabella Plantation can get over crowded in spring and summer, so try to visit on a weekday or in rainy weather. There is parking on Broomfield Hill and access from Richmond's main cycle path, or if you come on foot there's a big map to direct you at Ladderstile Gate.

royalparks.org.uk
Ladderstile Gate, Richmond Park, TW10 5HS

—

THE PHOENIX GARDEN

You'll find this small enchanted garden in an unlikely location in the heart of the West End, tucked between Charing Cross Road and Shaftesbury Avenue. It's a community garden run by volunteers to create a retreat from city stress and a habitat for urban wildlife. It is delightfully rambling, with nooks and crannies and three little ponds which are home to frogs and goldfish. There are benches dotted around the garden where you can sit and eat your sandwich or practise a few minutes of mindfulness meditation.

thephoenixgarden.org
21 Stacey Street, WC2H 8DG

—

INNER AND MIDDLE TEMPLE GARDENS

These peaceful, historic gardens are set within a cloistered enclave just minutes away from the cacophony of Fleet Street and Chancery Lane. They lie within the precincts of the Inns of Court – the professional associations for barristers in England and Wales. The three-acre Inner Temple Garden includes beautiful herbaceous borders, the remains of a medieval orchard and wide lawns for picnicking. In the Middle Temple garden you'll find rose beds, a lavender walk and an ancient mulberry tree in Fountain Court: a place to spend time appreciating the colours and fragrances of flowers. Those who work here may bustle by, but for the rest of us it's a wonderfully

restorative place within one of the busiest parts of London. Open to the public during lunch hours only (check the website for details).

innertemple.org.uk
middletemplehall.org.uk
Crown Office Row EC4Y 7HL;
Middle Temple Lane, EC4Y 9AT

—

QUEEN ELIZABETH HALL ROOF GARDEN

Climb up the yellow stairs next to the Queen Elizabeth Hall and you'll find yourself in a rooftop oasis, overflowing with wildflowers and vegetables. Hidden amidst the concrete landscape of the South Bank, the garden was created in partnership with the Eden Project, and is replanted each year by local community groups. Recently a woodland garden has been added. The original garden typically features over 100 species of British wildflowers, raised planters with vegetables like blue potatoes and hops, and bowers of scented climbers. The garden is open in spring and summer and can be a surprisingly quiet haven during the daytime, though it's popular and busy on warm evenings. You can bask in the sense of open space looking out over the river, or wander amongst the wildflowers, densely planted in the style of an English cottage garden, enjoying the profusion of scents and colours.

southbankcentre.co.uk
Southbank Centre, Belvedere Rd, SE1 8XX

—

KYOTO GARDEN, HOLLAND PARK

Japanese gardens are intended to be places for meditation and contemplation. Inside London's Holland Park is one such space: the Kyoto Garden was created to celebrate the 1992 Japan Festival in London. Here you can walk slowly around the pond, resting your eyes on carefully composed arrangements of rocks, water features and pruned trees or bushes. A small bridge next to a

waterfall is a lovely place to stop for a few minutes and practise mindfulness of sounds, or watch the koi carp swimming in the pond.

rbkc.gov.uk
Ilchester Place, W8 6LU

—

OPEN GARDEN SQUARES WEEKEND

For one weekend in June, around 200 gardens which are not normally open to the public unlock their gates to visitors. A weekend ticket allows you access to secret gardens across the city – these range from exclusive Belgravia gardens such as Eaton Square and Belgrave Square, to the seven-acre Ladbroke Square, minutes from Portobello Road. Other highlights have included allotment gardens, prison and school gardens, the Royal College of Physicians' medicinal garden, and even the gardens of No. 10 Downing Street. And, of course, with its June timing, you can feast your eyes on a colourful profusion of flowers – from rose gardens to wildflowers to kitchen gardens – and enjoy the greenery of orchards, topiary and enormous old trees.

opensquares.org

—

KEW GARDENS TOURS

The Royal Botanic Gardens, Kew, founded in 1759, is one of London's top visitor attractions. For Londoners, too, it is always worth a trip, to be wowed by nature's display of flowers and plants unique to each season. There are daily tours led by an enthusiastic band of volunteers, which are free with Gardens admission, including a general introductory tour, tours of the glasshouses and themed walks. Special longer tours and workshops have an additional charge. Here is a simple way to become more familiar with flower species which you may then recognise and enjoy more fully in your other travels around London.

kew.org
Richmond, Surrey TW9 3AB

Trees and woods

GREAT TREES OF LONDON

A good way to experience the calming effects of nature in the midst of a shopping trip or a working day is to visit some of the official 'Great Trees of London'. This A-list of 60 trees was set up after the 1987 storms which damaged so many of London's trees. The Berkeley Plane in Berkeley Square, Mayfair, was planted in 1789 and has a circumference of 1.8 metres, but it is surrounded by 30 other precious trees, all of which are at least 200 years old. The Marylebone Elm stands on the pavement next to a small 'Garden of Rest' at the north end of Marylebone High Street – 100 feet tall and 150 years old. It doesn't look so extraordinary but it is in fact a rare Huntington Elm, which not only survived the World War II bombing which destroyed the nearby church, but also Dutch Elm Disease in the 1970s, which wiped out three-quarters of Britain's elms. In Bloomsbury, the Brunswick Plane in Brunswick Square is another gorgeous, fat London plane planted by the Victorians, located near the centre of the garden. The oldest tree in London is said to be the ancient yew in the churchyard of St Andrew's, Totteridge, on Totteridge Lane. Experts say it could be around 2,000 years old, maybe even pre-dating Londinium itself!

ancient-tree-hunt.org.uk; treesforcities.org; *Great Trees of London* **(Time Out Guides, 2010)**

—

ANCIENT TREES: RICHMOND PARK

For a serious ancient tree pilgrimage visit Richmond Park, which boasts the largest concentration of ancient oak trees in London. Here you will find hundreds of giants – trees of legend. One of most magical is the Richmond Royal Oak, estimated to be 750 years old. To reach it from Richmond Gate, go up Sawyer's Hill, take the footpath along the north-eastern edge of Sidmouth Wood, follow it down the wood's eastern side, and you will find the tree near Queen Elizabeth's Plantation, north-west of Pen Ponds. It stands in its own clearing with a bench nearby – short, squat and gnarled, with a crack down the centre large enough to push inside. It measures over five 'adult hugs', with its enormous girth of 8.07 metres. Medieval, twisted and lumpy, it is the stuff of fairytales.

If you feel caught up in the frenetic pace of the 21st century, seek out these ancient trees to help put things in perspective, and inspire a sense of awe and mystery.

royalparks.org.uk
Richmond Gate, Richmond Park, TW10 5HS

—

NUNHEAD CEMETERY

Nunhead is a secret treasure of south London: a romantic and overgrown Victorian cemetery which is blissfully quiet despite being in zone 2 between New Cross and Peckham. Nunhead was one of seven Victorian cemeteries created around London in the mid-19th century to relieve the overcrowded churchyards of the city, and covers 52 acres on a hillside. Now it's an overgrown woodland with tumbledown gravestones and stone angels half-covered in ivy. There's a gothic chapel by architect Thomas Little, now minus its roof, and tilting monuments to eminent Victorian citizens. Quiet paths lead through woods of sycamore and ash, providing a haven for wildlife – 16 species of butterfly have been identified here. Near the top of the hill there's a bench with a stunning view across London including St Paul's Cathedral – a good place for quiet reflection.

fonc.org.uk
Linden Grove, SE15 3LP

—

SYDENHAM HILL WOOD

This 23-acre slice of woodland is the closest piece of ancient British woodland to central London. In the 13th century the Great North Wood covered 800 acres, and this is its last remnant, along with nearby privately owned Dulwich Wood. It is home to almost 200 species of trees and plants, including oak and hornbeam trees, wood anemone and lily-of-the-valley; and wildlife including woodpeckers, tawny owls and five species of bat. At Sydenham Hill Wood you can immerse yourself in the trees and let body and mind unwind: 'forest bathing' as the Japanese call it.

From Sydenham Hill station, cross College Road and take the path leading up the hill. Turn left on Crescent Wood Road and walk for about half a kilometre to reach the entrance to Sydenham Hill Wood. The woodland walk follows a disused railway line which has left romantic remnants including a tunnel and a raised footbridge. You can take a circular walk in the wood or continue on down oak-lined Cox's Walk onto the South Circular. From here, for a longer outing turn left for a kilometre's walk to Dulwich Park, where a stroll through the park will bring you to the Dulwich Picture Gallery.

wildlondon.org.uk/reserves/ sydenham-hill-wood-and-coxs-walk
Crescent Wood Road, SE26 6LS

—

EPPING FOREST

Epping Forest is London's largest open space, covering some 6,000 acres in east London, stretching into Essex. It's been forested since Neolithic times and is now a mix of ancient woodland, grassland, rivers and ponds. A fresh new visitor centre, The View, offers maps and information, including details of local walks like the 'holly trail' and the 'willow trail'. If you want to escape the maelstrom of London, immerse yourself in these ancient woods which were declared by Queen Victoria to be 'my people's forest'. Across the road in Barn Hoppitt you can linger and study some of the forest's most impressive ancient pollards – trees whose interesting shapes

were created by regular cutting to generate new shoots from the main trunk. Nearby Connaught Water is a pleasant spot for bird-watching and reflection.

cityoflondon.gov.uk/things-to-do/ green-spaces/epping-forest

—

Watery walks

REGENT'S CANAL WALK

Walking along one of London's old canal towpaths feels like entering into the slower pace of a different era. a watery haven from asphalt and traffic, yet completely urban. Regent's Canal, almost two centuries old, is a hidden artery linking some of London's most lively neighbourhoods. The two-mile stretch from Little Venice to Camden is often described as the most scenic, passing through Regent's Park and ending at the busy, colourful Camden Lock Market. Further east, I enjoy the slightly grittier urban landscape of another two-mile section, starting near Angel station at Colebrooke Row (N1 8AP), which winds by old industrial buildings, new architecture, gas works, locks, and houseboats. Just before Kingsland Road, there's a cluster of canal-side cafés. Stop at Arepa & Co (58A De Beauvoir Crescent, N1 5SB) to sip coffee in a hanging swing chair looking out on the canal. The Proud Archivist (2–10 Hertford Road, N1 5ET) is a café-restaurant-gallery-venue which aims to revive the traditions of the 17th- and 18th-century coffee house.

End the walk at Broadway Market, a hang-out for East End hipsters, with its food market on Saturdays and promenade of quirky independent cafés, pubs and shops – smaller and less frenetic than Brick Lane – where you can browse vintage clothes and bookshops. From here it's a 10-minute walk to London Fields rail station, or 15 minutes to Bethnal Green Tube.

canalrivertrust.org.uk
walklondon.org.uk

—

NEW RIVER WALK

The New River is a man-made channel created in 1613 to bring water from the River Lea in Hertfordshire to North London, and it still supplies drinking water to Londoners. Thames Water has created the footpath that follows the whole 45-kilometre length of the historic water channel. Many parts within London have been paved over, but there are stretches where the river runs above ground; one such is the linear park called New River Walk: a green sliver of landscaped riverside between St Paul's Road and Canonbury Road. Along this 1-kilometre stretch the path winds past a soothing blend of weeping willows, babbling water, ducks, coots and moorhens, overlooked by a mix of Islington villas and flats.

For a longer walk of 3 kilometres, start on Green Lanes 400 metres north of Manor House tube, from where the walk runs past the Stoke Newington Reservoirs, through Clissold Park, and down through Canonbury to finish at New River Head right next to Sadler's Wells theatre. Or for a serious 10-kilometre ramble, start at Highgate Tube and take the Parkland walk, which follows a disused railway line through beautiful woods, from which you can join the New River Walk near Manor House. These walks are a good opportunity to take a break from the busyness of the city and connect with the soothing, nurturing qualities of water and greenery.

shelford.org/walks/newriver.pdf
parkland-walk.org.uk
Wallace Road, Canonbury, N1 2PG

—

THAMES PATH

A walk along London's riverbank, however familiar, is always full of surprises. The Thames Path walk runs for 64 kilometres on both sides of the river, so there is always a new section to visit or a favourite part to rediscover. Even the popular stretch of the South Bank from the London Eye to London Bridge has its own ever-changing atmosphere, with its buskers, tourists, strolling Londoners and free festivals. I enjoy the quieter stretch which runs 2 kilometres eastwards from here, past the warehouses of Butler's Wharf and St Saviour's Dock, through Bermondsey to end at the Mayflower in Rotherhithe – the oldest pub on the River Thames (117 Rotherhithe Street, SE16 4NF). Or when you crave a dose of countryside, explore the western sections, from Hampton Court or Richmond or Kew. One of my mindfulness students writes: 'I like to explore the path along the river from Kew Bridge (west) towards Ham. Along here it is often very quiet and peaceful, and sometimes, when the river is low, you can climb down onto the banks and sit guarded from the path by the trees, and feel very much alone and at peace. This is a spot where I enjoy reflecting and meditating.'

walklondon.org.uk

—

WWT LONDON WETLAND CENTRE

A vast, tranquil paradise for birds and other wildlife, this 105-acre conservation area near the River Thames in Barnes is an ideal place for a few hours of mindful strolling. Pathways meander through a watery world of lakes, ponds and reedy lagoons. It was created in 2000 by the Wildfowl and Wetlands Trust on the site of four disused Victorian reservoirs, transformed by landscaping and joyfully reclaimed by nature. The London Wetland Centre provides a haven for over 180 species of bird each year, including wintering ducks like shoveler, teal and wigeon; warblers and wading birds in spring; summer migrants like sand martins; and elusive bitterns in autumn. Other wildlife to keep an eye out for include otters, water voles, bats, lizards, dragonflies and butterflies. The Centre runs a busy educational programme and is popular with school groups and families, but you can always find quiet spots for watching the wildlife, listening and reflecting.

wwt.org.uk
Queen Elizabeth's Walk, SW13 9WT

—

Group walks

INNER LONDON RAMBLERS

The Ramblers offers a chance to hook up with other walkers and discover new walks in the relaxing knowledge that someone else has worked out the route. The Ramblers is Britain's biggest walking charity and has nine groups in inner London. Some of these cover particular parts of the city, and there are also the age-based Metropolitan Walkers (20s–30s) and Capital Walkers (30s–50s). The London Strollers (all ages) takes a more leisurely pace, which may be conducive to mindful walking and enjoying the flora and fauna along the way. There are numerous walks on offer each week, all free, although they ask that you join as a member after the first couple of walks.

innerlondonramblers.org.uk

MINDFUL COMMUTING AND TRAVELLING

British people love to complain about the weather, and Londoners are no exception. However, after the cold and rain, our next favourite collective grievance is the trials of transport. London has a pretty good public transport system compared with many cities, but the sheer enormity of our metropolis means we can spend a vast amount of energy just getting from A to B. And even when we think we've left enough time to get to our destination, we are foiled by signal failures, engineering works, bus delays and traffic jams, which all wind us up and create a state of agitation.

Many of us spend a good chunk of each day travelling, so how could we turn that time into something that is more nurturing and less depleting? This chapter will explore ways in which you can make your journey an opportunity to be mindful. I'll suggest some short practices for the Tube, train or bus, involving bringing awareness to your own breath and body, or to some aspect of your environment. We can also experiment with other ways of calming the sense of rush and creating more enjoyment from the experience, such as leaving extra time or taking a different route.

Rather than wishing away the next minutes or hours wanting only to be at our destination, could we take the attitude that it's possible to appreciate the journey itself?

LEAVE EXTRA TIME

One of the simplest tips for enjoying London life without the constant sense of rush is to allow some extra minutes for every journey. I have to admit, I am not always the best person to give this particular piece of advice. My mother always told me to 'leave plenty of time, dear', and it felt like an act of rebellion to do everything as a last-minute dash. These days, my biggest downfall is the mesmerising power of my computer – it feels so compelling to answer that email or finish that task before I set off. Nine times out of ten it is not particularly urgent, and the feeling of satisfaction is far outweighed by the stress of running late for the duration of the journey.

When we do leave enough time, our travelling is transformed – we can relax and enjoy the ride. The inevitable delays of public transport are not really a problem, and if we do arrive early, we can take a few minutes to have a cup of coffee or practise mindful breathing, or sit watching the world go by as we wait for our friend or colleague to arrive – perhaps late themselves, out of breath and babbling excuses. We can smile and assure them soothingly that we were quite happy just sitting there, enjoying the luxury of a gap with nothing to do.

Try this: in the queue

Queuing time feels like dead time: at best we space out and get bored, at worst we stress and get agitated. But we can use the famous British queue as a chance to slow down and practise mindfulness. Whether we're at the bus stop, post office, bank or shop, we all know that thoughts of throttling the management or the people ahead of us will not help the queue move faster. Instead, take this moment as an opportunity for a break. Here you are, with nothing to do except stand here. Resist the urge to start playing with your phone, and take a few minutes to just be. Here is a breathing space you can practise in any queue:

- **Check in**: Feel your feet on the floor and the weight of your body. How is your body feeling at the moment – are you tense, relaxed, tired, aching, buzzing, agitated, calm? How is your mind – busy, anxious, dreamy, blank? Are you feeling any emotions – sad, angry, melancholy, excited, contented? See if you can notice how things are without trying to change anything.

- **Breathe**: Notice you are breathing. Bring your awareness up close to the physical sensations of breathing, wherever you feel them. Let the breath breathe itself and bring your attention to this natural rhythm. It may help to put a hand on your belly and feel the natural movement there, in the soft core of the body, away from the busyness of your head.

- **Expand your awareness**: From the narrow focus on your breath, broaden your awareness again to have a sense of your whole body and whatever you are feeling. Expand your awareness further to take in a sense of the environment and other people.

You could notice colours, textures, sounds, voices, the space around you. By taking this breathing space, you're not trying to change anything, you're giving yourself a few moments to be present and experience this place and time just as it is.

TAKE A DIFFERENT ROUTE

When we do the same journey every day, there's a natural tendency to go onto autopilot. Try making a change – small or large, it doesn't matter – to bring a sense of freshness to your route. When you have time, you could take the bus instead of the Tube, and sit on the top deck looking out of the window. Or you could take the Overground instead of the Underground, or work out a different route through an unfamiliar part of town. You could walk down a different street from usual and notice the shops and cafés. Or you could add a short walk to the journey, perhaps getting off the bus or Tube a stop early, arriving at your destination feeling more healthy and energised.

If you can create a route which involves crossing a park or the river, so much the better. The Royal Parks weaving through central London provide opportunities for a mindful walk which can sometimes be quicker than public transport, and certainly more rewarding – it's a great way to clear your head between appointments. For me, seeing the river is always refreshing and inspiring, and so I make a point of walking along it or crossing it whenever I can. If I'm travelling north or south of the river on the Northern Line, I often start or end my Tube journey on the wrong side so that I can walk across the pedestrian bridge and enjoy the view of St Paul's and the city skyline. Taking one of the Thames River Buses is another way to reconnect with the river – this service gives you a choice between the swifter commuter clippers or the more leisurely sightseeing ferries which will take you through the heart of London (tfl.gov.uk/modes/river).

Sometimes, though, we just need the fastest route, and although the Underground is much maligned, when parts of it aren't working it can make us appreciate that on a good day it hurtles us through great distances so quickly. Even a crowded Tube journey can be mindful, so here is an exercise to try when you are next on the Underground.

Try this: one-stop breathing space

Lots of people meditate on the Underground – I know this because many of them tell me they do. Sometimes you can spot them; they look just like anyone else who is resting or drifting off, except they might be sitting a bit more upright, and they might have a slightly more deliberate hand position – palms resting on their thighs or cupped in their lap. Don't worry, only a fellow meditator would possibly notice!

Here's a meditation exercise to try between two stations on the Tube route, to create a breathing space. You can do this with eyes open or closed, whatever feels comfortable.

- **Grounding**: As the doors close at the first station (accompanied by a 'beep, beep, beep'), take a few moments to feel the weight of your body and your connection to the ground. Whether you're sitting or standing, feel the contact of your feet on the floor. If you're sitting, feel your bottom on the seat.

- **Breathing**: As the train accelerates, bring your awareness to your breath. Feel the breath going in and going out. You could focus on the breath in the abdomen, expanding and falling back. Or you could focus on the sense of the out breath flowing from your nostrils into space. Wherever you feel the breath is fine.

- **While the train is at full speed, stay with the breath**. When the mind wanders off, gently bring awareness back to the breath. You will also be feeling the movement of the train; just allow your body to feel it without struggling against it. If you notice sounds – the train itself, people talking, announcements – see if you can let them be part of the environment.

- **Grounding/Expanding**: As the train enters the next station, gently start to relax your focus on the breath. You might still notice your breathing, but feel again your feet on the floor and the weight of your body. If your eyes have been closed, open them and notice your surroundings. Perhaps the feeling of the breath stays with you as part of your awareness.

Repeat this as often as you like. People in my classes often report that practising a 'breathing space' like this has been helpful for them in situations where they felt claustrophobic or panicky, such as on a packed Tube at rush hour. If you feel comfortable you could also settle in to a longer session of mindfulness of breath, or try mindfulness of sounds. An Underground advert of 1928 asked the readers: 'How does the Underground train run? Legato? Allegro con brio? Prestissimo? Rallentando?' You could close your eyes and pay attention to the changing sounds of the train – a kind of urban music with its own tones and textures. (For more on mindful listening, see Chapter 6.)

LONDON OVERGROUND

The map of the London Underground is ingrained in our city's consciousness, and many of us follow its well-worn routes out of ancient habit. But for many journeys, there's now the option to travel more swiftly and directly above ground, where you can enjoy views of some of the most intriguing parts of the city. In 2007, Transport for London took over the old Silverlink rail network with a mission to create a modern, efficient orbital railway – the final link was completed in 2012. The spacious, walk-through carriages with their cheerful orange branding create a generally less nerve-jangling experience than the Tube, and are perfect for people who feel claustrophobic on the Underground. The East London line links some of London's hippest areas – from Rotherhithe on the South Bank to Shoreditch, Hoxton and Dalston in the north – challenging the old dominance of the more commercial West End. Ride the Overground, put away your trashy free newspaper, and look out over rooftops, warehouses, alleyways and waterways, and the eclectic neighbourhoods of East London (tfl.gov.uk).

Try this: on the bus

Taking the bus, whenever possible, can offer a mindful experience as you pass through the city, discovering new neighbourhoods and travelling at a pace that feels more natural. London has one of the largest bus networks in the world, with 7,500 buses on more than 700 routes, and 90 per cent of us live within 400 metres of a bus stop, so wherever we are going, there is a way to travel at ground level. All we need to do is invest a few minutes to work out a route, either via the Transport for London website (tfl.gov.uk), or by pitching up at a stop and checking the maps.

Take a seat by the window on the top deck – if there is one, and if you can. Unless you have a physical reason not to climb stairs, it's a sorry moment when you're too tired, lazy or cool to enjoy one of London's great pleasures, the top of the double-decker bus. Try leaving your mobile and newspaper packed away and instead, dedicate the journey to looking. Watch the buildings, the shops, the street life as you pass by. If you're at the top, you have a perfect view of the bits we often miss – turrets, chimneys, roof gables, intriguing penthouses, views into flats, tops of trees, the sky, the clouds. Each time you find yourself drifting into thoughts that take you away, gently bring yourself back to the direct experience of seeing. Even if you're on a familiar route, each journey is different: a new mix of people on the street, a different cloudscape, a sunset over the common, an alleyway you never noticed before. Let your journey be an experience of presence, rather than absence; and of interest in the world, instead of indifference. You may find that you feel restored and grounded when you reach your destination.

ON FOOT

Get healthy, save money, reduce our carbon footprint – these are all good reasons for walking whenever we can. Walk or run to work in the morning and you will start the day feeling energised. (If all the way to work is too far, try getting off the bus or Tube a stop early and walking the last stretch.) Walk between meetings and you'll arrive refreshed and grounded, and less stressed by transport delays beyond your control. Walk around the block as a way of clearing your head at any time of day. Whenever you walk, it's an opportunity to become present in your body and aware of the environment, so that you can experience the city more fully.

Of course we all know that it's possible to walk without being all that mindful, especially if it's a route we can do on autopilot. It can take a conscious intention to let go of our mental chatter, and be present in the walking. A good way to do this is to bring our awareness into our feet and the physical act of walking. Once we are more grounded in the here and now, we can open our awareness to the rest of our senses and the environment.

Try this: mindful walking

If you've watched a small child learning to walk you know that it's a challenging and complicated process, but as adults we take it for granted. Here we will bring our awareness to this remarkable act that we do all the time without noticing. This is a practice you might like to try first at home, or outside on a quiet street or common where you are not worried that walking slowly and deliberately might look silly. Once you are comfortable with it, mindful walking can be done anywhere and at any pace.

- ◆ **Feel your feet**: Stand still for a few moments, with your feet hip-width apart, and feel the contact of your feet on the ground. Notice any sensations in the balls of your feet, the ten toes, the heels, the contact with your shoes. Feel the weight of your body. Try shifting your weight a bit forward, backward, left and right, and feel how the patterns of sensation change. We talk about someone having their 'feet on the ground', so explore what that is like, literally.

- **Take a step**: Transfer your weight onto your left leg, tuning in to any sensations in both legs and feet as the right leg empties out, the heel and foot come off the ground and move through the air. Place the right heel, then the foot onto the floor, maintaining awareness of the sensations as you transfer weight to the right leg and foot.

- **Start to walk**: Carry on walking, slowly, staying aware of the sensations in the feet as they make contact with the floor, and in the muscles of the legs. When you feel ready you can pick up the pace to a normal stroll. Look ahead, slightly downward, but there's no need to look at your feet – they know what to do. Each time your mind wanders off, gently escort it back to the sensations in your feet and legs.

- **Look up**: Once you feel grounded in your body and anchored in the present moment, feel free to raise your gaze and take in the environment. Notice what's around you, while still keeping some of your awareness in your feet. If your mind goes off into thoughts, come back to the feeling of your feet on the ground. When your mind is more steady, open your awareness again to the sights and sounds around you.

Once you get the hang of it, mindful walking can be done at any pace. Try experimenting: is it possible to be mindful even when you are going fast? Walking can be done as a mindfulness practice when you need a break, perhaps taking a mindful walk around the block. You can also bring this mindful quality into any journey on foot in the course of your day, using the act of walking as a way to bring yourself out of your head and into the present moment.

Find it on foot

London is far too big a city to know all its streets, unless you're a cabbie with 'the Knowledge'. Thankfully, to find your way on foot you don't need to be carrying an Ordnance Survey map and a compass, or even a London A–Z. Mobile technology makes it increasingly easy to find a good walking route wherever you want to go. Just be wary of over-using maps and apps so that you spend your whole journey with your face buried in your phone, missing the world you are walking through. I often still use my paperback mini A–Z because its physicality helps to keep me in the real world instead of the virtual one. When I do use my phone, I try to remember as much of the route as possible, so that I don't need to check at every corner.

Google maps will give you walking routes between any two points if you click on 'get directions' and select the walking icon (maps. google.co.uk). You can plan online, or use the mobile app. Walkit. com is an online route planner which does the same, with options to choose 'direct', 'less busy' or 'low pollution'. You can also find a circular route near any location, for when you'd like a walk for its own sake. Transport for London has a walking journey planner (tfl. gov.uk/modes/walking), or you can use the regular journey planner to find a combination of walking with other modes of transport. Edit the search based on how long you are prepared to walk, and choose 'slow', 'average' or 'fast' for a time estimate (journeyplanner.tfl.gov. uk). However, with all this support, don't forget the old-fashioned pleasure of walking without a map, following your nose, and discovering unexpected by-ways and alleyways. It's good sometimes to get lost in our own city! If you do have a smart phone, you can relax and get lost and bring out your phone when it's time to make your way home.

Pause: the red man

Here's a suggestion to help you be more mindful of the cityscape around you. When you're travelling on foot, how do you behave at traffic lights? Do you dash across as the green man turns to red, dodging oncoming traffic? Or do you shrug your shoulders and wait patiently. When we were working on a festival called 'Slow Down London', my friend and fellow meditator Annalie came up with the suggestion that the green man is one of the culprits of our speedy society. 'The green man always appears in the distance when you're approaching a crossing, egging you on to make a dash for it. You could just get there comfortably in your own time but his goading presence tempts you to quicken your step. And what of the red man – why doesn't he get the respect he deserves? Because he's dull and unpromising, that's why... But perhaps it's time we gave the red man a chance. He's had time to stand and survey the world, to take it all in. Beneath his rather severe surface lurks a kindly soul who just wants to keep you safe.'

When you reach a traffic crossing, why not make friends with the red man, and let him be a reminder to pause? Instead of being impatient for the green man, appreciate how the red man gives you a chance to stop, breathe, and look around. Notice the buildings, your fellow pedestrians, the cars and cyclists. Look up, at rooftops and the sky. Feel your feet on the ground. Take a breathing space, and by the time the green man eggs you on again, you may feel just a little more present and refreshed.

MINDFUL DRIVING

With our extensive public transport network, we often have better travel options than driving which don't involve clogging up the roads, polluting the air, and getting frazzled in traffic jams. When we do drive it can be stressful, but it can also be an opportunity for developing mindfulness. Obviously being behind the wheel is not a good moment to close your eyes and focus on your breath, or to look around so much that you neglect the road, but here are some other ways in which you could be mindful:

◆ When you get into your car, take a few conscious breaths before you start. And again at the end of your journey, when you switch off the engine. Feel your bottom on the seat. Notice if you are holding tension you could let go of.

◆ While you're driving, have some awareness of your body. Feel your hands on the steering wheel. Notice any tensions, such as hunching your shoulders, clenching your belly, gripping the wheel, or tightening your jaw. You may find that just by noticing you naturally relax a bit more.

◆ If you normally listen to the radio or music, experiment with switching it off and experiencing silence. Sometimes a break from advertising jingles, arguing politicians or pumping beats can be refreshing.

- Try slowing down. Most of us tend to push at the edge of the speed limit, or over. Driving just a few miles-per-hour slower can be more restful, better for fuel consumption, and makes little difference to our arrival time.

- Develop your awareness of the whole environment, on all sides and in the mirrors; in the near, middle and far distance. This spacious awareness helps us to be more responsive to potential hazards and more courteous to other drivers.

- Notice when you are getting irritated, competitive or aggressive. How does that feel in the body? When we are starting to get het up, by noticing fully what's happening, with good humour towards ourselves, we can often let it go. Try being generous to other road users even when others are not – you may find that you feel happier at the end of the journey.

ON YOUR BIKE

Cycling is an activity with a naturally mindful quality: we can't let our mind wander off too much from the present moment if we want to stay safe, and while we're on our bike we have to take a break from our phones and gadgets. It can be stressful, dealing with constant hazards such as unmindful drivers, fellow cyclists, or pedestrians stepping out into the road without looking. But at its best, travelling by bike feels healthy for body and mind, synchronising the two. We're gliding through the city with the wind in our face in a way that makes us feel alive. Outside the enclosed bubble of a car or bus, we can experience all of our senses more fully.

London's government has been trying to encourage cycling, with 'Cycle Superhighways' creating marked routes into central London. Thousands of 'Boris bikes', nicknamed after Mayor Boris Johnson, can be hired from docking stations around the city (tfl.gov.uk/barclayscyclehire). You can map cycling routes using the Transport for London journey planner (tfl.gov.uk), and the London Cycling Campaign also has a route planner which includes information on the busyness and hilliness of the route (lcc.org.uk). The National Cycle Network offers many kilometres of routes to lead cyclists around London in the safest and most pleasant way possible. As well as commuter routes into the city, there are some that are beautiful and ideal for a mindful weekend cycle. On the Sustrans website (the charity which developed the network) look for 'browse all routes' and select 'largely traffic free' or 'totally traffic free' (sustrans.org.uk).

For a mindful cycle ride, let go of straining to reach the top of the hill or thinking ahead to your destination and see if you can be with the feeling of your body and breath in each moment. You can feel the contact of your feet on the pedals, and your hands on the handlebars. At the same time, be aware of your environment, with a wide, spacious awareness that takes in the traffic, the other road users, the scenery, the sky. Sometimes if I'm cycling in wind and rain, I notice how much tension I'm generating by resisting the elements: gritting my teeth, hunching my shoulders and bracing my body. When I notice this, I see if I can relax and allow the cold to be cold, and the wet to be wet. After all, I will be warm and dry not so long from now, so I could enjoy how the ride brings me in full contact with the rawness of the weather, whatever that may be.

MINDFUL GUIDE

NUMBER 11 BUS

Any bus journey can be mindful, but this one is particularly good for sightseeing, not only for visitors to the city, but for Londoners with a destination on this route or who are willing to enjoy being a tourist in their own city. The number 11 is among the oldest bus routes in London, introduced in 1906, although its route has changed a few times. Its current route is as good as that of a sightseeing bus – and saves you the £20-odd fare! – taking you through the heart of the city and past many of London's great landmarks. Get on at Liverpool Street station and take a seat on the top deck. You'll go past the Bank of England, St Paul's Cathedral, the Royal Courts of Justice, Somerset House, the Savoy Hotel, theatres on the Strand, Trafalgar Square, the Houses of Parliament, Westminster Abbey, New Scotland Yard, Sloane Square and then down the King's Road into Fulham, ending at Fulham Broadway Tube. Or do it the other way round, and from Liverpool Street you could finish your journey at one of the nearby cafés of Shoreditch.

tfl.gov.uk

—

OPEN-TOP SIGHTSEEING BUS

If you're a visitor to London and you'd like a live guide to explain what you're seeing (and if cost is not an issue), several companies provide sightseeing buses. The open-top buses let you feel the weather – rain or shine – and a sense of being present in the city without the barrier of windows. Tickets give you the flexibility to 'hop on, hop off', and some packages include a river cruise or walking tours. You can shop around for discounts, and do look out for whether you are getting a live tour guide or a pre-recorded commentary.

theoriginaltour.com
eng.bigbustours.com
hoponhopoffplus.com

GOLDEN JUBILEE BRIDGES

After a day in the city, crossing the River Thames is refreshing: a feeling of washing the crowded mind with space and light and the fluid quality of water. We can easily forget the great river; I make a point of crossing the Thames as often as possible, especially on the new 21st-century footbridges which have reclaimed the river for pedestrians. The Millennium Bridge, with its view from Tate Modern across to St Paul's, is a wonderful walkway. Waterloo Bridge, while carrying road traffic, has a wide pavement which makes it a good walking bridge. For me, the ultimate London bridge is the Hungerford Bridge, or more precisely the two cable pedestrian bridges which flank it, officially called the Golden Jubilee Bridges. From one side you can see the Houses of Parliament and the London Eye, and the other side gives spectacular views across to St Paul's Cathedral and the City. If you're travelling anywhere near Waterloo or Charing Cross, allow an extra ten or fifteen minutes and exit on the opposite side of the river. Take a mindful walk across the bridge, opening all your senses to the watery world of the Thames and the city skyline.

Golden Jubilee Bridges, WC2N 6PA

—

RIVER BOATS

Travelling on the Thames gives you a chance to connect with the soothing, spacious qualities of the river, and to see London from a different angle. The faster River Bus services, run by KPMG Thames Clippers, are used by commuters between Putney and Woolwich, with discounts for Oyster card holders. When you have time, there are more leisurely 'river tours' run by several different operators, including 'hop on, hop off' services and sightseeing cruises with live commentary on the sights. Some offer lunch or afternoon tea on board. Tickets are sold from offices at the pier – Westminster, the London Eye and Embankment are popular starting points – or sometimes on board the boat.

tfl.gov.uk/modes/river/

—

EMIRATES AIRLINE

One of London's most unusual ways to travel is the UK's first urban cable car, which runs between North Greenwich and the Royal Docks. It offers views over the 02 Arena towards the city in one direction, and down towards the Thames flood barrier in the other. This trip is a chance to regain a sense of space in built-up London and enjoy the cityscape from a bird's-eye perspective. Oyster card holders receive discounted fares.

emiratesairline.co.uk

—

WALK LONDON

Walking – not to get somewhere, but for the sheer pleasure of it – can be just as enjoyable in London as in the countryside. Walk London

has developed a network of seven long-distance walking routes and shares these through maps and directions on the website. You can pick a random section for a Sunday stroll, or complete a whole walk in segments over time. The walks include canal and river routes (as described in Chapter 2), such as the Thames Path and the Jubilee Greenway, which runs in part along Regent's Canal. There are also a couple of huge circular walks: the 126-km Capital Ring, which takes you through some of London's greenest suburbs, and the 245-km Loop (London Outer Orbital Path), which encircles London like an 'M25 for walkers'. The Green Chain passes through dozens of woods and parks in south-east London, and the Lea Valley Walk follows the Lea Navigation towpath through remains of our industrial past. The Jubilee Walkway is a more central walk, taking in the city's most iconic landmarks. It takes a bit of planning and map-reading to do one of these walks, but once you're on it, you will be rewarded by a perfect opportunity for mindful walking, discovering parts of our extraordinary city which you may never have known.

walklondon.org.uk

—

CYCLE TRAILS: THE WANDLE

A surprising, mainly traffic-free cycle route in south London is the Wandle Trail. This 20km route follows the River Wandle from its mouth at the Thames in Wandsworth, and heads south-east towards Croydon, taking in green spaces and hidden parts of the city. Highlights are Merton Abbey Mills, a former textile works which once housed William Morris's factory, and Morden Hill Park, a tranquil National Trust estate. Wilderness Island near Carshalton is a haven for dozens of bird species.

merton.gov.uk

—

CYCLE TRAILS: LONDON'S DOCKLANDS AND LEA VALLEY

This watery ride covers a 42km route, mainly traffic-free, from Greenwich in the south of London to Tottenham Marshes in the north. On the way, you pass through the Isle of Dogs, Victoria Park, Hackney Marshes, Walthamstow Marsh Nature Reserve and the Lea Valley Regional Park. The route is lined with a wonderful mix of post-industrial landscapes, river boats and nature reserves. Canalside pubs such as the cluster near Hackney Wick offer stopping points for rest and reflection with a drink or food.

sustrans.org.uk

—

ARCHITECTURE AND ART: MINDFUL SEEING

Mindfulness brings us to our senses: by slowing down and noticing more, we rediscover the freshness of our sense perceptions. The combined input of our senses is often overwhelming, so to cultivate mindfulness we can practise bringing our awareness to one sense at a time. We don't have to block out the other senses, but we can adjust our attention so that the main focus is on seeing (this chapter), listening (Chapter 6), tasting (Chapter 7) or the physical sensations of our body (Chapter 8). We can step out of autopilot and develop our interest in simple experiences that we've been taking for granted.

Seeing is the richest and most dominant of our senses. Each moment we are taking in vast amounts of visual information – most of which we screen out. Research shows that the retina communicates to the brain at roughly 10 million bits per second, but the brain can only process about 1 per cent of this information. On our familiar walk to the station or bus stop, we take in a tiny fraction of what is actually there, editing out what we perceive is not useful to us.

When we're in an unfamiliar city on holiday, we may find we notice so much more: all the details of traffic signs, shop windows, architecture and street fashion seem so interesting and fresh. What would it be like as a traveller in our own city, noticing the richness of the detail? Now and then you may have the experience of suddenly noticing something in your neighbourhood for the first time – an unusual building, a quirky shop, a mysterious alleyway. Suddenly you are awakened from your fog of familiarity – has this been there all along? We can nurture this freshness of experience by cultivating mindfulness of our visual surroundings.

One thing I find helpful is simply to look up. It's so easy to hurry along with eyes on the pavement, or to stay at shop level, attention hooked by printed signs and commercial messages. On the high streets of most London neighbourhoods, if you look up above the shop fronts you will find elegant terraces, eccentric turrets, crumbling gargoyles, intriguing penthouses, faded advertising, fresh graffiti art. It's also one of the delights of the double-decker bus to glide along above street level – so instead of playing with our phones, we can take a seat on the top deck and look out the window, as children instinctively do.

Try this: mindful seeing

Choose a location for a 5- or 10-minute walk, perhaps around the block near your home or office.

* Start your walk by 'grounding yourself' in your own body and the present moment: literally feeling the contact of your feet on the ground. Notice the weight shifting from one foot to the other as you walk.

+ Now open your awareness to the act of seeing. Let your main focus of attention be on the visual field, noticing the shapes, colours and textures of the things you pass. Notice the tendency to go off into thoughts and judgements about what you see ('I wonder who owns that car ... '; 'They really should paint that wall ... '). Thoughts will certainly arise, but see if you can let them go a little, and come back to the direct experience of seeing.

+ Try for a while having a wide focus, like a film camera panning to set the scene, and opening up to your peripheral vision. Then try focusing in on small details, perhaps slowing down or stopping to look at the light shining on a leaf, or the texture of a fence.

+ If it's helpful, you could imagine you are a painter, sculptor or photographer (that is, if you are not one already), keeping your eyes open for interesting subjects and angles.

EVERYDAY ARCHITECTURE

In *Mindful London* we are especially interested in exploring ways to be mindful which are part of daily life and don't have to take us out of our way. If we can become more aware of the fabric of the streets of London, it can wake us up from our stupor and return us to the here and now. Our historic city can itself become an art gallery that we are constantly moving through, full of interesting shapes, textures and colours – man-made as well as natural.

London's built environment is an extraordinary hodgepodge – a 'city of villages' with erratic street patterns and buildings from every period. We can lament the lack of cohesion, or delight in the unpredictable mix of styles around each corner. London's streets radiate a sense of history that can wake us up to a bigger perspective. These buildings have stood through wars and economic depressions, immense social changes, watching as neighbourhood fortunes rise and fall. Just as an old gnarled tree has a presence which challenges us to step out of our petty anxieties, so can London's buildings – if we let them.

As we walk down the street, when we are not in a complete mental fog, we are often mesmerised by shop signs and billboards. The printed word tends to grab our attention above other kinds of input. As a result we can let ourselves be bombarded by endless commercial messages, while missing the greater part of our environment. Try looking above the shop fronts, or behind them. Are there intriguing alleyways, or fancy brickwork, or turrets? Are the buildings all of one era, or an eclectic mix of periods? Are there colours and shapes to interest your eyes?

If you look out for distinctive period features it can help you to notice your surroundings more fully. In the Georgian squares of Bloomsbury, Hackney or Kennington, stop for a moment to rest in the symmetry and harmony that radiates from the buildings. Walking through the sweeping white and cream Regency terraces of Mayfair or Pimlico, enjoy the graceful shapes of columns, pilasters and fanlight windows. In countless Victorian neighbourhoods keep an eye out for decorative flourishes adorning simple terraced houses. Even on my familiar south London street I can still come across details I haven't seen before: an Italianate arch, a porch tiled with terracotta flowers, a stained-glass window, little faces peering from painted foliage above a doorway.

Some more recent architecture has been controversial, but if we look freshly even at the buildings we think we don't like, we may find there is more to interest our eyes than we expected, whether 30s mock-Tudor, 60s Brutalism or 80s post-modernism. And now gleaming glass creations like The Shard are reaching into the sky – love them or hate them, they demand our attention and invite us into a different sense of vertical space. On your travels, see if you can appreciate each new streetscape, noticing intriguing juxtapositions of varying styles.

GHOST SIGNS AND STREET ART

As well as noticing buildings, we can keep an eye out for other creative expressions of Londoners past and present. As you travel through the city, look out for the faded remains of advertisements that were once painted by hand on the brickwork of buildings. Some advertise local businesses such as ironmongers or piano sellers; others big brands like Hovis or Gillette who paid for 'posters' to be painted across the UK. Stoke Newington and Hackney are particularly rich with these signs, faded but still clinging to the walls. These 'ghost signs' are an intriguing reminder of the past and of the sign-writer's craft, which fell into decline with the advent of printed billboards (ghostsigns.co.uk).

Painting on walls is, of course, very much alive in the form of street art – from community murals to spray-can art. East London has exploded with street art over the last decade, particularly the areas around Old Street and Shoreditch, and into Hackney. If you're in the area, keep an eye out for witty, beautiful and provocative artworks on walls, doorways, shutters and in alleyways. To see some of the

most interesting work, you can take a walking tour with a guide
who knows about the newest artists, artworks and techniques.
You'll come away with a greater appreciation for the ever-changing
creative spirit of the city as expressed on its walls.

BIRD'S-EYE VIEWS

Seeing can involve different kinds of focus: narrow and wide. We
can zoom in on a detail, reducing our sensory input to one thing
and giving it our full attention. Often this is a good way to slow
ourselves down when we're overwhelmed. We can also take the
opposite approach, like a camera with a wide-angle lens, taking in
the whole view at once. This also helps to shift our mind-set, in a
slightly different way. We may be feeling claustrophobic, caught
in rumination over our plans and worries, which seem to fill the
universe with their importance. Taking a bigger view, quite literally,
can help us to see things in perspective and remember there is a
whole world out there that we can open our senses to. We might
relax a little with the knowledge that it's not revolving entirely
around us.

Seeking out panoramic vistas is thus a wonderful way to develop
a greater understanding of our cityscape, and at the same time
to give ourselves this sense of space and perspective. Most of us
instinctively love a high view, but perhaps we forget to indulge this
pleasure in our own city. London offers many stunning viewpoints,
from old favourites like St Paul's dome and the Monument to newer
vistas from the London Eye and The Shard. For a cheaper experience
there are free vantage points like Parliament Hill, or for the price of
a drink or a meal you can enjoy stunning views from Centre Point

and the Tate Modern. These bird's-eye views stop us in our tracks and give us a new angle on our city and our place within it.

SLOW ART

Let us turn now from the streetscapes of London and step inside the city's great art galleries, whose whole *raison d'être* is 'mindful seeing' – or at least, so we might hope. However, many Londoners look at art primarily in the context of blockbuster exhibitions, and having paid our ticket fee we try to get our money's worth by racing through the galleries ticking off every notable painting. We may spend more time reading the caption than looking at the work itself. Researchers in museums have found that 30 seconds is the average time people spend in front of a work of art. An artist took days, months or years creating this painting, and yet we find it hard to spare it even a minute of our time.

When we spend less time reading, and more time looking, the art rewards us by revealing things that we miss at first glance. You may feel that you should know a lot about the artist, their technique, the context, and so on, before you can understand a painting or sculpture. Of course, these things are interesting and can be helpful, but if you look first, you might be surprised at how much you discover for yourself instinctively, even without a lot of expertise. When my children were small, I sometimes helped chaperone them on school trips to art galleries, where someone from the education team would sit them all down in front of a painting. I was astounded at the insightful art criticism coming out of the mouths of five-year-olds: they could naturally see what the artist was trying to do when they were guided to really look. We can do the same, spending time looking, noticing the textures and colours and how the composition is put together, or just drinking in the overall feeling of the artwork and the reaction it provokes. We may go back out into the city seeing everything a little bit differently, as if through the eyes of that particular artist.

Try this: slow art

You can enjoy 'slow art' any time by walking into a gallery or museum when you are passing by, and spending ten or fifteen minutes with just one painting, maybe two. The National Gallery, National Portrait Gallery and the British Museum are obvious choices because they are excellent for this: located in areas that most of us visit periodically for shopping or work, and thankfully free of charge. Another approach is to make an outing of it with a friend, partner or group, perhaps to the Tate Modern or Tate Britain or a smaller gallery. We included this with great success as part of a 'Slow Club' some years ago, and now there is a global Slow Art Day, with organised events in many cities, including sometimes London (slowartday.com).

When you arrive at the gallery, agree where to meet up again in one hour's time. During that hour, allow yourselves to look at a maximum of three artworks. With a bit of wandering time in between, that will mean spending at least 15 minutes with each artwork. Choose whatever you are drawn to, or you could also challenge yourself by picking a work you find difficult. Don't let yourself look at the caption until almost the end. Look at the artwork itself. You don't have to worry about who it's by, or what you are 'supposed' to be looking at. Just look. At the end of the hour, meet up with your friend(s) and discuss your experience over tea or coffee; then you could go back and revisit one or two of the artworks together if you like. You can also happily do this exercise alone – just be strict with yourself about the timing as it may well feel very slow indeed! But each time you feel you are bored or have seen everything, look a bit longer and you may find that new details and connections reveal themselves.

MINDFUL GUIDE

Architecture and street art

BEDFORD SQUARE AND THE OPEN GARDEN SQUARES

Next time you're shopping on Tottenham Court Road or Oxford Street, take a break from the maelstrom and step into Bedford Square, one of the best-preserved Georgian squares in London, near the British Museum. The pavements just outside the garden are unusually wide and spacious: perfect for a short meditative walk. In 1775 it was the first London garden square to be designed with an imposed architectural uniformity, with each side treated as a single unit. This continuous 'palace front' made each of the four terraces look like one large country house with a central pediment and flanking wings. It set the style for garden squares in London. See if you agree with a description of 1783, which

claimed: 'it is without exception the most perfect square in town. The regularity and symmetry on the sides, each of which is adorned with a central building faced with stone and enriched with pilasters and a pediment, the great breadth of the pavements, and the neatness of the iron-rails... render it superior in everything but magnitude to any square in Europe'. The garden inside the square is not normally open to the public, but like all the Bloomsbury Squares can be visited during Open Garden Squares Weekend, the second weekend of June every year (opensquares.org).

bloomsburysquares.wordpress. com/bedford-square
Bedford Square, WC1B 3DN

—

A REGENCY WALK

Many of us visit Regent's Park for a lunchtime stroll or to see the zoo, and perhaps take for granted the beautiful terraces on its fringes. In 1811 the Prince Regent's leading architect John Nash created a master plan for the area as a vast rounded park surrounded by palatial terraces.

If you start at Regent's Park Tube you can first drink in the elegant sweep of Park Crescent, with its perfect colonnade of doubled Ionic pillars all the way round, and the nearby facing terraces of Park Square. Combine a park stroll with popping out to look at the nearby rows of houses, which include Cornwall, York and Ulster Terraces to the south, and Hanover Terrace and Sussex Place to the west. Don't miss Cumberland Terrace on the east side – a block of 31 houses in grand neo-classical style, enlivened with sculpture – and nearby Gloucester Gate. From the park's inner circle, you can see the two Nash villas still standing (out of 56 planned and 8 built): St John's Lodge and The Holme. Within the park, Queen Mary's garden has London's largest collection of roses, with approximately 12,000 varieties: a chance to luxuriate in your sense of smell, especially in early June,

when the blooms are at their most beautiful and fragrant.

royalparks.org.uk
Regent's Park, NW1 4NR

—

THE NATURAL HISTORY MUSEUM BUILDING

One of London's most distinctive Victorian buildings is the Natural History Museum, so popular as a holiday playground for children that we may forget to look beyond the dinosaurs to the extraordinary architecture of the building itself. Designed by Alfred Waterhouse and opened in 1881, it is one of Britain's most striking examples of Victorian Romanesque architecture. It resembles a cathedral with its high spired towers, ornate facade and impressive entrance with nested rounded arches. The ceiling of the grand central hall is intricately painted with flora and fauna, and the building is extensively decorated inside and out with terracotta carvings of living and extinct animals. Here you can bask in the full glory of high Victorian design, all the better to notice the more modest echoes we see reflected in the houses and mansion blocks which many of us still live in today. For a quieter visit, avoid school holidays, unless of course you are bringing children.

nhm.ac.uk/visit-us/history architecture
Cromwell Rd, London SW7 5BD

—

LEIGHTON HOUSE MUSEUM

A less-known Victorian gem is Leighton House, in Holland Park, home of the artist Frederick, Lord Leighton (1830–1896). Built for him as a studio-house, it grew into a private 'palace of art' filled with paintings and sculptures by Leighton and his contemporaries, and is decorated on every surface. The highlight is the stunning Arab Hall, modelled on a Sicilian

palace, with its golden dome and intricate mosaics. It's a beautiful, contemplative space, lined with a sea of turquoise and blue Islamic tiles, where you can hear the trickling sounds of an indoor fountain. The unique collection of Syrian tiles was begun by Leighton on a trip to Damascus in 1873, and added to by friends including the explorer Richard Burton. A place to linger and enjoy a rich feast of the senses: a Victorian-English version of Eastern Persian grandeur.

rbkc.gov.uk/museums
12 Holland Park Road, W14 8LZ

—

THE BARBICAN: URBAN VILLAGE

The Barbican was voted 'the ugliest building in London' in 2003, but this vast complex has been softened over time and is now Grade 2 listed and increasingly appreciated by Londoners. It is restful sitting on the terrace by one of the rectangular ponds,

with water fountains playing.
Here you are secluded from busy
streets by the courtyard layout,
influenced by the Georgian
squares of Bloomsbury. Your view
is of the medieval St Giles' church
juxtaposed with the Barbican's
modernist flats, the crenelated
roof of the church echoed in
castle motifs throughout the
estate. While the Barbican is
known primarily as a brutalist
development, if you take one of
their regular architectural tours
you'll hear about a more complex
set of influences during the long
30 years from the architects' first
stages of planning in the 1950s to
the opening in 1982.

The Barbican Centre is Europe's
largest multi-arts venue, with a
dazzling range of music, dance,
film, theatre and art on offer in its
many spaces. Above the Centre is
a two-storey glass atrium housing
a hidden tropical oasis with
2,000 species of tropical plants
and trees, along with finches
and fish. It's the second-largest
conservatory in London, after Kew
Gardens, and is open to the public

on Sundays – though check the
website as it is sometimes closed
for private events.

barbican.org.uk
Silk Street, EC2Y 8DS

—

THE GEFFRYE MUSEUM

The Geffrye Museum is dedicated
to showing how English homes
and gardens have reflected social
change over the past 400 years.
A series of eleven period rooms
let you steep yourself in the style
and furnishings of each era, from
an oak-panelled 17th-century hall
to a 1990s loft apartment. We can
be more awake to London's built
environment across the centuries
when we have a feel for the
sensibilities of each era and the
ways that people have chosen to
arrange their living spaces. There
are also period gardens reflecting
four centuries of middle-class
domestic gardens. These are
lovely places for a mindful stroll
in their own right, but also provide
an opportunity to learn about

changing fashions in layout and planting so you can notice and appreciate these features in other gardens around the city.

geffrye-museum.org.uk
136 Kingsland Road, E2 8EA

—

OPEN HOUSE LONDON

Each year in September the Capital's largest festival of architecture and design offers free access to over 800 buildings across the city. They range from historic landmarks to the latest new architectural projects, with many architects giving talks and tours of buildings they've designed. It's a wonderful way to engage with both historic and contemporary architecture, and to develop a better appreciation of the city.

londonopenhouse.org

—

STREET ART TOURS IN EAST LONDON

Street art is constantly appearing and disappearing, so a good way to see interesting things might be to take a walking tour. Street art can be found right across London, but Brick Lane and nearby streets like Redchurch, Grey Eagle, Grimsby and Hanbury usually have a particularly high concentration of artworks – large and small. Several local organisations run tours which are aimed at both Londoners and visitors, led by guides who are passionate about the street art scene and are sometimes artists themselves. They can tell you about the artists and their techniques, from stencil and paste up to freehand painting, and they know the newest locations. Alternative London also offers tours by bike, and workshops if you're up for trying a bit of art yourself.

Street Art London has also come up with a free app which lets you find the latest work on your own smart phone, and is regularly updated. You can browse the map finding pinpoints near your location, or filter by artist, each with a biography, so you can get to know the individual artists and their styles. But as with any app, do use it sparingly, and not as a replacement for actually looking! Armed with a little more knowledge, you may find yourself stopping to notice and appreciate a lively art scene you might have passed by before, or dismissed.

streetartlondon.co.uk
shoreditchstreetarttours.co.uk
alternativeldn.co.uk

—

Viewpoints

THE LONDON EYE

When I first went up in the London Eye, I was astounded by the view of London's chaotic architecture from above, and particularly how many landmarks were not quite where I expected them to be in relation to each other. Cities built along a straight shoreline or on a grid are easy to get to grips with, but the curving Thames means it's hard to orient ourselves in any simple north–south way, or to hold an overall picture of the geography of the city. The Eye attracts crowds in high tourist season, but during the winter months you can more easily turn up and get a ticket. The slow pace of the turning wheel lulls you into a restful, meditative state, so you can give your full attention to the view.

londoneye.com
Westminster Bridge Road, SE1 7PB

—

PARLIAMENT HILL

This north London hill is much loved for having one of the best free views of London's skyline. It's an area of open parkland in the corner of Hampstead Heath, at a height of 98 metres. From here you can see out across the trees to landmarks like St Paul's, the Gherkin, The Shard and One Canada Square.

cityoflondon.gov.uk/hampstead
Hampstead Heath, Parliament Hill,
NW3 2SY

THE SHARD

Travel 72 floors up to the top of this gleaming icicle of a skyscraper for panoramic views across the whole of London. Tickets are pricey, and some people would argue that the view is more interesting from lower, more traditional vantage points like St Paul's, where you still feel part of the city instead of soaring above it. The View from the Shard is almost twice the height of any other viewing platform in London, and on a clear day you can see for up to 40 miles.

the-shard.com
32 London Bridge St, SE1 9SG

—

ST PAUL'S CATHEDRAL

Climb to the top of this historic building for the iconic view of London from the Golden Dome, with views of the City district, the Thames, and all the great landmarks – except St Paul's itself, of course. Admission price includes entry to the Cathedral floor, crypt and the three galleries in the dome (Whispering, Stone and Golden), as well as multimedia guides and guided tours. A chance to enjoy both the spaciousness of a big vista and the beautiful, restful proportions of Christopher Wren's architectural masterpiece.

stpauls.co.uk
St Paul's Churchyard, EC4M 8AD

—

MONUMENT

Christopher Wren's stone monument to the Great Fire of 1666 is one of the cheapest ways to get up high above the city. Some views are now obstructed by taller buildings but there's still a good panorama. You could take the 311 steps as an opportunity to practise mindful stair-climbing, feeling your feet on each step and enjoying the climb instead of rushing to get to the top.

themonument.info
Monument Street, EC3R 8AH

THE PIPERS CENTRAL LONDON MODEL

The next best thing to a trip up the Eye or the Shard – and perhaps better for sheer understanding – is to visit the Pipers Central London Model. This is a 12-metre-long model, built to scale at 1:1500 by 15 model makers over nine months, and regularly updated. You can see the low-rise nature of the historic city, all in grey, and the speed of the new high-rise development, with major recent buildings and proposed buildings highlighted in white.

This stunning model is the centrepiece of New London Architecture, which was founded in 2005 to promote awareness and debate about London's built environment. Spacious galleries display exhibits on the latest development plans in London's 33 boroughs, and showcase new architecture, from modest home extensions to ambitious office blocks. It's free to visit, with a café where you can take a break from the mayhem of nearby Tottenham Court Road. They also run talks and walking tours of 'new London'. With a little understanding of what's happening in architecture and planning, we may find ourselves more aware and engaged about the changes happening in our streets as we go about the city, watching new buildings sprouting and old ones regenerating.

**newlondonarchitecture.org
The Building Centre, 26 Store Street, WC1E 7BT**

—

Small galleries

THE COURTAULD GALLERY

The Courtauld Gallery bills itself as one of the finest small art museums in the world, and rightly so – almost every artwork is a masterpiece. The scale is conducive to mindful looking; it's less daunting than The National Gallery, and about the right size for a visit of a couple of hours. Tucked away in a corner of the grand, neo-classical, 18th-century

Somerset House, many Londoners never get around to visiting it. The elegant, high-ceilinged rooms create a restful setting for the paintings, which include famous and familiar Impressionist and Post-Impressionist works by Monet, Cezanne, Renoir, Gauguin and Van Gogh. Other highlights include some Renaissance gems and a striking collection of German Expressionists. There's a café with pleasant outdoor seating, and across the courtyard in the south wing of Somerset House are several more cafés and bars.

courtauld.ac.uk
Somerset House, Strand,
WC2R 0RN

—

SERPENTINE GALLERIES

Combine art and nature with a walk through Kensington Gardens to visit the Serpentine Galleries, where you'll find a changing programme of contemporary art exhibitions. The original Serpentine is a bright, spacious gallery with full-length windows looking out onto grass and trees: a beautiful place for looking mindfully at art. In the summer months (June–October) on the gallery's lawn you can visit the Serpentine Pavilion, which is commissioned annually from international architects and always offers a weird and wonderful exploration of the possibilities of architectural form.

Five minutes' walk away, across a bridge, you'll reach the Serpentine Sackler Gallery, converted from an 1805 gunpowder store. Stop for a drink or meal in The Magazine – the landmark restaurant and social space created by architect Zaha Hadid, with its undulating, wave-shaped white roof, glass walls and sinuous columns. It feels a bit like being in a 60s vision of the future; as one critic wrote, 'a survivor of a forgotten world's fair – let's say an astrophysics pavilion'. You can sip your coffee from perfect designer cups, and look out into the greenery of the park or up at the oval skylights.

serpentinegalleries.org
Kensington Gardens, W2 3XA

—

OCTOBER GALLERY

The October Gallery exhibits
contemporary art from around the
globe and has played a pioneering
role in bringing worldwide attention
to leading artists from Africa, Asia,
Oceania, and the Middle East,
as well as Europe. The gallery
describes itself as promoting the
'Transvangarde': the shape of
things to come across the planet.
It is located on the ground floor of
an elegant three-storey Victorian
building in Bloomsbury, with a
secluded garden-courtyard and
café – a lovely spot for tea and cake.
The curators have a keen eye for
outstanding contemporary art, and
if you stop by for any exhibition
you are likely to see work that is
unusual, intriguing and beautiful,
and which gives a glimpse of the
world viewed from a different angle.

octobergallery.co.uk
24 Old Gloucester Street, WC1N 3AL

WHITECHAPEL GALLERY

The Whitechapel was founded
in 1901 as one of London's first
publicly funded galleries, and
has premiered a stunning roster
of world-class artists such as
Picasso, Pollock, Rothko, Kahlo,
Freud and Gilbert & George. More
recent exhibitions include works
by leading contemporary British
artists such as Gillian Wearing
and Sarah Lucas, and the summer
London Open showcases new
artists from across the city. The
gallery space was doubled in 2009
as the result of remodelling by
Belgian architect Robbrecht en
Daem, who created a beautiful
environment lit by skylights.

The Whitechapel has a lively
outreach programme, connecting
itself to the local East London
community, and hosts many
smaller free exhibitions including
lots of photographic work. The
small but bright restaurant has a
1950s Scandinavian feel, and serves
an interesting menu of modern
European food. Make sure you
look up at the copper weathervane

on the Gallery roof, designed by Vancouver artist Rodney Graham. It depicts the artist as the 16th-century scholar, Erasmus, seated backwards on a horse while reading *The Praise of Folly*, too absorbed in his book to notice the journey: perhaps a parable about mindfulness?

whitechapelgallery.org
77–82 Whitechapel High Street,
E1 7QX

—

Slow artworks

SLOW VIEWS OF LONDON: NATIONAL GALLERY

Any artwork can be a candidate for the Slow Art approach; here are a couple that also offer views of London to enrich our vision of the city. A small but delightful painting from the west side of London is Albert Sisley's 'View of the Thames: Charing Cross Bridge' (National Gallery, Room 43). Sisley was a leading figure in the Impressionist movement, who lived in France but painted this on a visit to England in 1874. It's a lively river scene with steamboats, St Paul's rising in the background, pale light and the energy of Sisley's brushwork. In the room next to Sisley's painting (44) is the famous 'Thames below Westminster' by Monet: a misty scene with jetties casting broken shadows on the river, and the ethereal shapes of the Houses of Parliament looming behind.

nationalgallery.org.uk
Trafalgar Square, WC2N 5DN

—

THE ARCH, KENSINGTON GARDENS

Sculptor Henry Moore must be the artist who has had the greatest impact on London's public spaces, with some dozen creations dotted around the city. The Arch was presented by Moore to the nation in 1980 – two years after his 80th-birthday exhibition at the Serpentine Gallery – for placement nearby in Kensington Gardens, on the north bank of the Long Water. Sadly, it was disassembled in 1996 because of instability, and languished in storage until 2012 when it was restored to its full glory. It's a beautiful six-metre-high sculpture made from creamy-white Italian travertine stone weighing 37 tonnes. Although the fencing unfortunately doesn't allow for looking at its curves and shapes from all angles, the Arch still frames a lovely view of water, ducks, greenery and Kensington Palace in the distance.

Other Henry Moore sculptures across London include Three Standing Figures in Battersea Park (west end of the lake, SW11 4NJ); Two Piece Reclining Figure 5 in the grounds of Kenwood House (Hampstead Lane, NW3 7JR) and Knife Edge Piece next to the Houses of Parliament, often used as a prop on news broadcasts (Abingdon Street Gardens, SW1P 3JY). Moore's sculpture has become so familiar as to breed

complacency, but if we look at it freshly we may appreciate the powerful physicality of these monumental pieces set within London landscapes, showing us both nature and the human form in a new light.

royalparks.org.uk
Long Water, Kensington Gardens,
W2 2UH

—

ASIA GALLERIES, V&A

Spending time with beautifully crafted objects can be very restful, especially objects which reflect a contemplative or meditative dimension of experience. The ground floor of the V&A contains a number of skilfully curated galleries – transformed in recent years with the support of wealthy donors – which illuminate the arts of Asian cultures. The Jameel Gallery displays Islamic art from the 8th century AD, from metalwork to ceramics to tilework and the world's oldest-dated carpet. You can let your eyes roam over the exquisite geometrical and floral designs which are often used to symbolise the indivisible and infinite nature of the divine.

In the nearby Robert H N Ho Family Foundation galleries, Buddhist sculpture from across Asia is shown in a spacious, naturally lit environment with minimal use of cases. The sculptures range from the 2nd to 19th centuries, and come from India, Sri Lanka, Tibet, Nepal, Thailand, Burma, Java, China and Japan. Artists from across these great swathes of time and space have wrestled with stone, metal and wood to depict versions of the same figure: the Buddha, or 'awakened one', who was said to have discovered how to live a life that was fully awake. Here we can perhaps take inspiration for living our own mindful or 'wakeful' lives from the sublime smile on the faces of these meditating Buddhas.

vam.ac.uk
Cromwell Road, SW7 2RL

—

Mindful seeing

THE BIG DRAW
One way to look more freshly at the world is to try drawing it ourselves: the act of putting pencil to paper teaches us to observe and develop our own way of relating to the visual world. The Big Draw is a month-long annual festival, encouraging people of all ages to discover the pleasure of drawing. Events across London take place at partner venues like the V&A, Queen Elizabeth Olympic Park, The National Gallery, the Houses of Parliament, the Wallace Collection and the Royal Academy of Arts. As well as traditional drawing with pencil, there has been printing, mosaics, mobiles, sandpainting, graffiti, wire sculptures and fire drawing. The festival is run by the Campaign for Drawing each October.

campaignfordrawing.org

—

PHOTOGRAPHY COURSES

Photography is another way to nurture our interest in the visual environment, and the freshness of seeing. We can use it as a way of deepening and sharpening our observation, rather than allowing the view through the lens to become a replacement for looking with the naked eye. City Lit, the centre for adult learning, offers a wide range of courses for all levels, including special London-oriented courses such as 'London's urban landscape', 'Photographing London's architecture', 'Photographing London at night' and 'Street fashion photography'. Classes take place in their Covent Garden studio, and other locations such as Blackheath. The London School of Photography also offers weekend and evening courses at their Soho site. For an urban adventure, photographer Anthony Epes runs workshops called 'London at Dawn' which start an hour before sunrise during the spring and summer months. These on-location courses focus on how to shoot the city at the most beautiful time of day, and on 'the ability to observe the world around you with a heightened awareness and insight'.

citylit.ac.uk
lsptraining.co.uk
londonatdawn.com

—

RESTFUL
SPACES

London is Europe's most populous city: in the 2011 census we numbered 8.17 million. On average, there are 12,331 of us per square mile, more than ten times the number in any other British region. If we commute at rush hour, we feel that density of human population very palpably, joining the wave of bodies teeming through the gates of a Tube station, or squashed onto the bus or train. Mindfulness can be very helpful in these moments, enabling us to go with the flow, rather than tensing up and creating irritation or panic. We can use techniques like the 'breathing space' to help us relax with these challenges to our personal space (see Chapter 3). However, we may find that we are more able to be buoyant in the midst of urban life if we also give ourselves regular breaks from the crowds. We can seek out places where we can be alone within a greater sense of stillness and space, even if briefly as part of a hectic day.

TIME ALONE

Some of us are rarely alone; perhaps we share a flat, work in
an open-plan office or spend our evenings socialising. And yet,
despite its population density, London is said to be the loneliest
place in the UK, with more than half of us (52 per cent) saying we
experience loneliness. Of course, there are very real problems of
social isolation, particularly amongst older people, but there is also
a cultural debate to be had about the whole idea of 'loneliness'.
The philosopher Paul Tillich wrote that 'Language... has created
the word "loneliness" to express the pain of being alone. And it has
created the word "solitude" to express the glory of being alone.'
We've created a society which is terrified of spending any time
alone, and where our technology encourages us to fill every space.
If we have a spare moment we immediately need company in the
form of entertainment: we plug in our music, turn on the TV, text
our friends or surf the web. Understandably, if we sit down to
practise mindfulness, or even take a few moments in a quiet place,
we may feel nervous, bored and even afraid.

How can it be that we value individualism and autonomy so highly,
and yet we are terrified of being alone with ourselves? Artists and
thinkers over centuries have sung the praises of solitude as the
wellspring of creativity and the source of personal strength. The
Catholic mystic Thomas Merton wrote of solitude as 'a deepening
of the present'. Others, like the poet Rainer Maria Rilke, offer
recognition of the challenges: 'It is good to be solitary, for solitude
is difficult; that something is difficult must be a reason the more for
us to do it.'

Mindfulness offers us a way of rediscovering the nurturing quality of solitude. In the city we can be so busy interacting with others that we lose touch with ourselves. In solitude, we discover a still, centred quality which helps us not to be buffeted about by the needs and demands of other people. We can gently train ourselves in being comfortable when we are alone. We don't have to retreat to the wilderness, but we can take moments here and there to duck out of the maelstrom. If you're someone used to frenetic social activity, it could be a matter of balancing social life with an afternoon or evening to yourself. Or if you have a job that involves constant meetings and communication, can you find a place at lunchtime for a break from colleagues? Whether you make the time for some formal mindfulness practice, or just take ten minutes to be alone, you can start to feel more centred in yourself and to enjoy being in your own company.

FINDING QUIET PLACES

We talk about getting some 'peace and quiet': solitude and silence are often linked in our minds. As well as taking a break from other people, we may long for a break from the noise of city life which can jangle our nerves. London can be noisy, but there are also many parts of the city that are surprisingly peaceful – not just parks and churches, but ordinary residential neighbourhoods. If your area is more sonically hectic, make a point of seeking out some quieter places. Many of the green spaces described in Chapter 2 are ideal places to connect with natural sounds – birds, water, wind and rain. The silence of indoor spaces has a different quality – bright or muffled, hushed or echoing. Visit the churches and other peaceful buildings described in this chapter for a short time out, or a quiet spot to practise mindfulness.

Silence is 'an endangered species' according to Gordon Hempton, who travels the world recording natural sounds and campaigning for quiet. He defines real quiet not as the absence of sound, but the absence of noise. Quiet is a 'think tank of the soul'. But for those of us who spend much of our time surrounded by noise, silence – like solitude – can be disconcerting. An Australian study of 580 undergrads found that constant exposure to background media had made them afraid of silence. 'When there is no noise in my room it scares me', 'I found the library was so quiet that I couldn't concentrate properly!'

If you find silence unsettling, try starting with short periods of quiet. The sensory bombardment of the city keeps us in a state of hyper arousal, on constant alert against potential dangers. We are trapped in the 'fight or flight' mode: our sympathetic nervous system is fired up, our adrenaline is pumping, our heart rate and blood pressure increase in preparation to fight or run from a threat. A period of quiet and stillness will let the parasympathetic nervous system come into play, relaxing blood vessels, decreasing our heart rate, and reducing the release of the stress hormone cortisol, which dampens the body's natural defences. Our body and mind can reset themselves and that buzzy, jangly feeling begins to lessen.

Try it in small doses: turn off the radio while cooking. Walk to the station without your iPod on. You may find that you start to enjoy periods of time without all that stimulus. Slowly, silence begins to feel nurturing and comforting.

THE PLEASURES OF BROWSING

Browsing in a library or bookshop is an old-fashioned, restful pastime which many of us have abandoned in these days of online shopping. It's one thing to order a specific book from the web, but it's another experience to walk slowly down the aisle of the library, looking at the titles and pulling one down from the shelf. Or to go into a bookshop without an agenda, simply picking up books that appeal to you as they catch your eye. Browsing in a bookshop can be a bit like fishing is for some people: an excuse to hang around doing not very much, in a relaxing way. If you step off a crowded West End street into one of London's big, eclectic bookshops such as Waterstones, Daunt, Foyles or Hatchards, it's like entering an oasis. Here you can linger in fiction, or amble through architecture, philosophy or film like a traveller on holiday in a foreign city.

We might argue that reading itself is not exactly about mindfulness: it is not generally inviting us to be present in this current place and time, but to journey with the author to other places. Yet in many ways it can have a mindful quality, encouraging us to be fully focused on the narrative, and on one thing at a time. Different kinds of reading can be more or less focused or fragmented. Sometimes I go through phases where I read too many newspapers and magazines in a superficial way, scanning bits here and there, searching for some kind of entertainment without finding satisfaction. At other times, when I'm in the midst of a novel or a good non-fiction book, my mind feels nourished by the depth of focus, as I immerse myself fully in the storyline and the author's voice.

Poetry is possibly one of the most mindful arts: it often captures the magic of everyday life in a way that is beyond more literal or analytic ways of thinking. Poetry is about noticing. Picking up a good poem we may feel the freshness of sense perceptions, the infinite weather patterns of human emotion, or the timeless quality of the present moment. Visit the Saison Poetry Library at the Southbank Centre, or dip into the poetry section of any bookshop or library. And when you're sitting on the Tube running your eyes over random adverts, look out for the Poems on the Underground, which invite you to slow down, read carefully, and nourish the mind with more meaningful words. A good poem will stop you in your tracks, and entice you out of autopilot to see the world in a new light.

REFLECTIVE SPACES: CHURCHES AND TEMPLES

Traditionally, over the centuries, one role of religion has been to act as a counterbalance to our everyday concerns. Spiritual traditions have encouraged us to go beyond our immediate worries to reflect on the bigger picture and what life is all about. In Britain, for one day a week the shops were traditionally closed to ensure that we put aside work for a day of rest and church-going. Now, on a Sunday morning, we're more likely to be rushing around Sainsbury's doing the weekly shop. In a largely secular society, one reason for the growing popularity of mindfulness may be a sense that we need to put on the brakes, and balance our constant activity with some of the more reflective space which used to be built into the rhythm of our communal life.

The presence of churches on every high street is a reminder that we once had a different sense of priorities. We don't have to be Christian, or religious, to appreciate the energy and aspiration which went into creating these steeples that rise above the rest of the neighbourhood, and the beautifully proportioned spaces below them. We can take them as reminders to stop, reflect, and connect with a deeper sense of the present, in whatever way we understand that. Many churches are, of course, active places of worship, full of services and events, especially on Sundays. They may have other priorities besides quiet reflection, including preaching the gospel and caring for isolated or impoverished members of the community. However, on a typical weekday in London – say on a break from work – it's likely that your local church will be quiet and that you are more than welcome to come in for a peaceful stroll, to admire the architecture, or to sit and do mindfulness practice.

As a historically Christian country we have at least one church in every neighbourhood as part of our shared cultural heritage, and they are open to all. I've picked out a few London churches for the Guide section which I find particularly beautiful or noteworthy, but you can make your own local discoveries. I also mention a couple of temples of other faiths which welcome visitors, and if you come from another faith background you may have access to places of worship which offer the same opportunity to step out of the daily maelstrom and be quietly present.

HISTORIC HOUSES AND
OTHER RESTFUL SPACES

A day out at a stately home or historic house is a traditional English pastime that is not always a restful experience, especially if we find ourselves rushing through crowded rooms ticking off 'must-see' items of furniture and artwork, or stuck with our nose in a guidebook. However, if we can visit when it is quieter, and spend time absorbing the atmosphere, it can connect us through all the senses to a different age and a slower pace of life – or at least slower for the leisured classes who inhabited these houses. As we steep ourselves in the colours, shapes and textures of another century, it can shift our perspective so we are less obsessively caught up in our own current projects and plans.

Some of our great museums and galleries are not only places to enjoy art, but have become our secular cathedrals, where we can step inside for a few minutes and let our minds relax into a different sense of space. The Great Court at the British Museum and the Turbine Hall at Tate Modern are two such places on a grand scale, but you may have your own local favourites amongst the many museums and galleries around the city.

Spas

Sometimes it's good to take a complete holiday for both the body and mind. When we're not due for a longer break, a few hours or a day at a spa can help our frazzled nervous system to reset itself. Spas can be expensive if we go for all the extras and treatments, but a basic day or evening entry can be just as effective. Here we can relax in a rotation of sauna, whirlpool, steambath and pool until time slows right down. London has several affordable spas, such as Porchester Spa and the Spa London centres, which are run on a not-for-profit basis. You can also surf the web for spa-break deals at some of the more luxurious hotels and health clubs (spabreaks.com).

A trip to the spa can be a popular day out for friends together, or for hen parties – a companionable way to pass the time. However, for a fully mindful experience, try a day on your own and let yourself luxuriate in the physical sensations of the body, and feel the nurturing qualities of heat and water. In solitude you can let go of chatter and allow your mind and body to settle into a different, more leisurely pace.

MINDFUL GUIDE

Bookshops and Libraries

WATERSTONES

Waterstones' flagship store on Piccadilly is Europe's biggest bookshop, with six floors of books in an Art Deco building which once housed the Simpson's department store. There is ample space for dipping into the tables of books laid out according to enticing themes, or to browse through eight and a half miles of shelving, and then take time to read in the sofas and chairs set out for this purpose. The 5th View cocktail bar and grill is a relaxing place for a drink, with views out over the rooftops towards the Houses of Parliament. The Gower Street store is the leading branch for academic titles, and there are some 50 smaller branches in greater London.

waterstones.com
203/206 Piccadilly, W1J 9HD

DAUNT BOOKS

Daunt Books is one of the most distinctive bookshops in London: an original Edwardian shop with long oak-panelled galleries and a glass conservatory ceiling which lets in natural light. The soothing atmosphere invites leisurely browsing. Daunts is especially known for its selection of travel books, stocking a vast collection of guidebooks, maps, language books, travelogues, history and culture arranged by country and region. It also has a well-picked selection of literary fiction, biography, poetry and most other genres. They have four more branches around the city, but visit the original in Marylebone if you can.

dauntbooks.co.uk
83 Marylebone High Street,
W1U 4QW

—

HATCHARDS

Hatchards is the oldest surviving bookshop in London. Established in 1797, and retaining some of its old-fashioned atmosphere, it is now owned by Waterstones. As with Daunt Books, the dark-wood panelling and period furnishings give it a calming gravitas which invites us to slow down the pace and browse. Walking in off Piccadilly is like a break from the 21st century, entering an era when we had all the time in the world for the quiet companionship of books. The ground floor can get busy with tourists, but there are five floors altogether, and helpful staff who let you sit and read. It's especially strong on history, arts and fiction, and hosts high-profile book readings and signings.

hatchards.co.uk
187 Piccadilly, W1J 9LE

—

FOYLES

Foyles on Charing Cross Road is a London institution; one of the few multi-department independent bookshops left in the city, and one of Europe's largest. It was once famous for its arcane chit payment system and idiosyncratic book shelving, but since 2000 it has modernised and innovated. Its specialties include the largest foreign language selection in the UK, and a music department with sheet music, and classical and jazz CDs and vinyl, inherited from the acquisition of Ray's Jazz shop in 2002. In 2014 Foyles moved from its home of many decades next door into the former Central Saint Martin's building at 107 Charing Cross Road, which features a tall central atrium from which you can look out over a sea of books on every floor. On the top floor is a café with views over the rooftops of Soho, and space for a full programme of exhibitions and author events. Foyles has also expanded to open smaller shops across the city, including branches in the Royal Festival

Hall and Waterloo and St Pancras International stations.

foyles.co.uk
107 Charing Cross Road, WC2H 0EB

—

LONDON REVIEW BOOKSHOP

The London Review Bookshop sees itself as a modern version of London's long-lost literary coffee-houses, where you can drink tea, eat cake and peruse the books within an atmosphere of gentle intellectual babble. The Cake Shop features delicious cakes, a small savoury menu, jasmine and other fragrant teas, and good espresso. The book selection is curated thematically and includes many older titles, rather than just piling up the latest bestsellers. The shop aims to replicate the ethos of the *London Review of Books* by being intelligent but not pretentious, with a strong selection of contemporary fiction and poetry, world classics, and thought-provoking non-fiction. Located

right near the British Museum, it's a haven from the bustle of the West End.

londonreviewbookshop.co.uk
14 Bury Place, WC1A 2JL

—

THE SCHOOL OF LIFE

The School of Life is much more than a bookshop; their Marchmont Street shop sells a selection of thought-provoking books on the ground floor while workshops, lectures and courses take place in the classroom downstairs. They describe their mission as 'developing emotional intelligence through the help of culture', and they engage leading thinkers to teach innovative courses on work, relationships, community, money and other practical themes. This is a space to develop mindfulness in the broadest sense, by reflecting on how to make good choices and lead a more fulfilled life.

theschooloflife.com
70 Marchmont Street, WC1N 1AB

THE IDLER ACADEMY

Like the School of Life, the Idler Academy is a bookshop on the outside but you can step through this gateway into a particular vision of the world, as envisioned by Tom Hodgkinson, founder of *The Idler* magazine and author of *How to be Idle*. Here you'll find classes in slow, old-fashioned subjects and skills like calligraphy, astronomy, English grammar and playing the ukulele. The bookshop itself is a calm, quiet place, which serves coffee and cake and has a small 'medieval' garden.

idler.co.uk/academy
81 Westbourne Park Road, W2 5QH

collections by leading poets to magazines, audio and video. The library aims to stock all poetry titles published in the UK, along with a selection of world poetry. There's an exhibition space and a few tucked-away desks where you can read quietly. Membership is free on display of current ID with proof of address. The library is not only a peaceful physical space, but somewhere you can explore how poetry can lead you to more spacious places in your own mind and experience.

poetrylibrary.org.uk
Level 5, Royal Festival Hall,
Belvedere Road, SE1 8XX

—

SAISON POETRY LIBRARY

On the top floor of the Royal Festival Hall is the UK's major library for modern and contemporary poetry, with over 200,000 items dating from 1912 to the present. The collection ranges from hand-printed pamphlets to

—

NATIONAL ART LIBRARY

Located within the V&A museum is this vast reference library of art and design books. It covers the fine and decorative arts of many countries and time periods, from prints and drawings to textiles, fashion, furniture and ceramics

– all the areas for which the V&A museum is famous. It's also home to the V&A's collection on the craft of book-making, with books that are works of art in themselves. The library is quiet and airy, with a beautiful Grade II-listed interior and large windows overlooking the garden. A lovely space for serious study or to indulge a private passion for any aspect of our material culture and arts. Membership is free on display of current ID with proof of address.

vam.ac.uk/nal
Cromwell Road, SW7 2RL

—

Reflective spaces: churches and temples

SOUTHWARK CATHEDRAL

Borough Market and the stretch of the Thames west of London Bridge has become a packed neighbourhood popular with both Londoners and tourists. Step out of the busyness into Southwark Cathedral to immerse yourself in a sense of space and visual richness. Take a few minutes for reflection, or go for a stroll amidst the soaring Gothic arches. Southwark has only been a cathedral since 1905, but as a church it goes back over 1,000 years, to the foundation of a priory in 1106. The building retains the basic Gothic structure built between 1220 and 1420, while the nave is a late 19th-century reconstruction by architect Sir Arthur Blomfield. It's an active church, with a reputation for inclusivity in a fast-transforming neighbourhood. On Monday lunchtimes and Tuesday afternoons you can catch free organ recitals and concerts, with paid concerts from high-profile ensembles at other times – check the website for news. The north-side extension built in 2000 includes a café which is a relaxed place for lunch or tea.

cathedral.southwark.anglican.org
London Bridge, SE1 9DA

—

ST BARTHOLOMEW THE GREAT

'Great St Barts' in Smithfield is one of London's oldest churches, founded in 1123, and a deeply atmospheric place for wandering and contemplation. Entering from West Smithfield, you reach the church through a rare 16th-century timber gatehouse. The church itself has the most significant Norman interior in London, which miraculously survived the Great Fire of 1666 and both World Wars. It has been used as a location for films such as *Four Weddings and a Funeral*, *Shakespeare in Love* and *The Other Boleyn Girl*. There is an entry fee for tourists, but no charge to come and sit quietly in the side chapel, in 'prayer or private devotion'. The 15th-century cloister hosts a café serving tea, coffee, cakes and snacks, soup and pies, and a range of monastic beers.

greatstbarts.com
Cloth Fair, EC1A 7JQ

—

ST ETHELBURGA'S

This little medieval church looks incongruous in the midst of the bustling City, tucked in between office buildings, with the glittering Gherkin looming behind. The church was rebuilt after near-demolition by an IRA bomb in 1993, retaining some of its original arches and brickwork within a simple, modern interior. It is no longer a functioning church but instead has been turned into a Centre for Reconciliation and Peace, holding workshops and talks on themes like conflict training and environmental consciousness. Behind the church is a 'secret garden' with flower beds, a fountain and Arabic screens, against a backdrop of rising skyscrapers. In the next little courtyard is 'The Tent' – a 16-sided Bedouin-style tent in woven goats' hair, with low benches and rugs made in places of conflict around the world. Come and sit quietly in the tent during opening hours, or attend one of their events in the main church, which include world music and storytelling. You can visit on Fridays from 11am to 3pm, and at other times by prior arrangement.

stethelburgas.org
78 Bishopsgate, EC2N 4AG

—

ST STEPHEN WALBROOK

This stunning church in the heart of the City was the parish church of the great architect Sir Christopher Wren (who rebuilt 52 London churches after the Great Fire of 1666) and is considered by many to be his finest work. You step inside to be bathed in space and light, in a vast, perfectly proportioned classical space; white everywhere, with light from clear glass windows. The building's centrepiece is its Renaissance dome, with ornate white plasterwork, surrounded by arches and Corinthian columns which create an impression of circularity within a rectangular building. Light pours down through the dome's central lantern onto

a massive stone altar by Henry Moore, surrounded by curved pews. This is a place to clear your head of stress and re-connect with a sense of simplicity and harmony. There are regular free lunchtime organ recitals and classical music concerts, if you would like to add sonic harmony to your experience of the physical space.

ststephenwalbrook.net
39 Walbrook, EC4N 8BN

—

ST ETHELDREDA'S

This gem of a chapel is Britain's oldest Catholic church, built in 1290 as a London base for the Bishops of Ely. St Etheldreda was a princess from East Anglia who became a nun, founded a religious order, and was quite a revolutionary, setting free the bondsmen on her lands and living a life of austerity. Her chapel is simple and beautiful but hardly austere, with its magnificent stained glass. The west window has been said to be the largest stained-glass window in London, and is notable for its graceful early 13th-century tracery, which survived the bombing of the church in the Second World War. It is tucked away on a gated road just off Holborn Circus, so pop in here for a respite from noise and traffic. There is regular Mass sung in Latin on Sundays and in English on weekdays at 1pm.

stetheldreda.com
14 Ely Place, ECIN 6RY

—

BHUDDAPADIPA TEMPLE

Hidden away in the very English suburbs of Wimbledon, and set within four acres of land, is a traditional Thai Buddhist temple. Visitors are welcome to stroll in the tranquil grounds, which include an ornamental lake with three small bridges, peaceful groves and a flower garden. You may encounter a monk or two, as the temple is an active monastery, and they are generally happy to chat and answer questions. The

temple was built in 1982 following Thai architectural principles and is ornately decorated in gold and red. Inside, you can reflect on murals depicting the Buddha's life, and gold and bronze Buddha statues brought from Thailand. Sundays are the busiest days, attracting London's Thai community for talks and shared food; so for a quieter visit choose another day. Classes on meditation and Buddhism are offered regularly.

buddhapadipa.org
14 Calonne Road, Wimbledon Parkside, SW19 5HJ

—

BAPS SHRI SWAMINARAYAN MANDIR

This stunning feat of architecture is the largest Hindu temple outside India, and a sight worth travelling to Neasden to experience. The *mandir* (temple) was built according to the traditional Hindu discipline of *Vastu Shastra*, or the 'Discipline of Sacred

Architecture', which is based on principles of harmony between the human building and the cosmos. Every detail of its proportions and alignments is designed to create spaces that are conducive for worship and reflection. Over three years thousands of tons of Bulgarian limestone along with Italian and Indian marble were shipped to 14 locations around India to be hand-carved by 1,500 artisans. The 26,300 pieces were then sent to London to be assembled in one giant jigsaw puzzle and completed in 1995.

Enter through the cultural centre, or Haveli, with its intricate wooden carving, then pass through inner courtyards into the white marble sanctum of the temple itself. Here you can enjoy the exquisite marble carving of the columns and arches, and the floral-patterned dome. Take time here for your own meditation, or you are also welcome at the midday *arti* or 'ceremony of light' in which lighted wicks are waved before the sacred images. Non-Hindu visitors are very welcome but check the website for dress code, be prepared for security

checks, and avoid Hindu festivals like Diwali if you'd like a quiet visit.

londonmandir.baps.org
105–119 Brentfield Road, Neasden,
NW10 8LD

—

Historic houses

OSTERLEY PARK AND HOUSE

Located in 140 acres of parkland in suburban Isleworth, west London (now bisected by the M4), Osterley House began as a red-brick Tudor house built in 1576 by Sir Thomas Gresham, founder of the Royal Exchange. It was acquired by the Child family, established bankers, and in 1760 the architect and designer Robert Adam remodelled it into a Georgian palace. The house contains Britain's most complete examples of Adam's work, with its elegant neoclassical interiors, wonderful plasterwork, rich colour schemes, and even some original Adam furniture. Wander in the grounds which include 18th-century gardens, ornamental lakes and an uncultivated meadow which is home to bluebells and butterflies.

nationaltrust.org.uk/osterley-park
Jersey Road, Isleworth, Middlesex
TW7 4RB (sat nav TW7 4RD)

—

FENTON HOUSE AND GARDEN, HAMPSTEAD

This 17th-century merchant's house is filled with beautiful, peaceful objects: oriental and European porcelain, 17th-century needlework, Georgian furniture and early keyboard instruments. There are occasional concerts on the harpsichords and virginals which are part of the collection. The house is set in lovely walled gardens which include a kitchen garden, a sunken rose garden, topiary and a 300-year-old apple orchard. The balcony offers views across the city, taking advantage of the house's high Hampstead vantage point.

nationaltrust.org.uk/fenton-house
Hampstead Grove, NW3 6SP

CHISWICK HOUSE

Chiswick House is a splendid neo-Palladian villa, never intended as a private residence but commissioned by the Earl of Burlington as an architectural experiment and a gallery to display his art collection. Rest your eyes on the classical proportions of this building and linger over artworks, decorative ceilings and stonework. The gardens, restored in 2010 at the cost of £12.1 million, are considered the birthplace of the English Landscape Movement and have inspired countless gardens from Blenheim Palace to New York's Central Park. It is a lovely place for a mindful stroll, taking in the lake, Italian gardens, a cascade, raised terraces, 18th-century statues and a large conservatory with a collection of rare old camellias.

chgt.org.uk
The Estate, Chiswick House,
Middlesex W4 2QN

—

ELTHAM PALACE AND GARDENS

This extraordinary south London palace combines medieval and Tudor grandeur with 1930s Art Deco decadence. Once the childhood home of Henry VIII, the medieval Great Hall remains, but for many the biggest attraction is the Art Deco palace built next to it by the wealthy Courtauld family. The furniture and décor seem right out of a classic film, from the impressive entrance hall to glamorous bathroom – a chance to luxuriate in 1930s elegance. There's a tea room and 19 acres of gardens to wander in, with a dry moat, rock gardens and beautiful herbaceous borders.

elthampalace.org.uk
Court Yard, Eltham SE9 5QE

—

Other restful spaces

THE TURBINE HALL, TATE MODERN

The Turbine Hall is like a great cathedral to our industrial past, a vast space five storeys tall which once housed the electricity generators of the old power station. Now it is a temple to contemporary art and hosts some of the most memorable site-specific works by leading figures of the art world. A sponsorship deal with Hyundai Motors has ensured that these high-profile commissions will continue until 2025. As you enter the hall, your mundane worries are dwarfed by a sense of vastness and timelessness. And with each new work you can immerse yourself in the creative vision of the artist as they rise to the challenge of filling the space with forms and ideas.

tate.org.uk
Bankside, SE1 9TG

—

THE GREAT COURT, BRITISH MUSEUM

For a breathtaking experience of light and space, there is no building to match the Great Court. It can swallow up coach-loads of school children and tourists and still radiate a white, peaceful spaciousness that is balm for the spirit. It is hardly a quiet space, and yet the babble of crowds dissipates into waves of muffled echoes. Designed by Foster and Partners and opened in 2000, it is the largest covered square in Europe. Its undulating glass canopy opens the building to the sky and clouds above, shimmering and changing with the skyscape. Everything is pleasing to the eye: the crisscross patterns of the roof, the round Reading Room, the curving staircases, the Grecian columns. If you have the time, pop into one of the galleries to look at one or two of the Egyptian sculptures in nearby Room 4, or the Buddhas in Room 33 at the far end, or the African pots and masks in Room 25 down the stairs. You can stop for a coffee in one of the Court Cafés, eat lunch in the Great Court restaurant, or stroll around the courtyard absorbing the atmosphere.

britishmuseum.org
Great Russell Street, WC1B 3DG

—

Spas

SPA LONDON

Spa London is a non-profit social enterprise which provides spa facilities at an affordable price, including aroma steam rooms, tepidarium, caldarium, laconium, sauna, hammam, plunge pool, along with massages and other treatments. Their first spa, York Hall leisure centre in Bethnal Green, is housed in a grand neo-Georgian building which was first opened in 1929 and is known internationally as a boxing venue. The building has recently been given a £4.2m makeover, restoring the interiors and bringing the leisure facilities up to date. In addition to the main sports hall – still home to boxing – York Hall houses a 33-metre, 8-lane pool which is spacious for lane-swimming. There's also a fitness centre and studio, and the original Turkish baths in the basement have been transformed into the spa and treatment centre. There are now five further Spa London locations around the city. Visit the website for times of male, female and mixed sessions.

spa-london.org
Old Ford Road, E2 9PJ

—

PORCHESTER SPA

Porchester Spa is another leisure centre which first opened in 1929 and has also been extensively refurbished recently. Located westward across town in Bayswater, it has a 30-metre swimming pool and smaller teaching pool, and afterwards you can relax in London's oldest spa. The building and the spa itself retain its original 1920s grandeur, including the pale Portland Stone interior, sweeping arches, high ceilings and green and white tiles. The pool has lovely roof windows and other decorative

features, and is not usually crowded. For the spa choose from men only, women only or mixed sessions.

better.org.uk/leisure/porchester-centre
Queensway, W2 5HS

—

AMIDA SPA, CHELSEA

Located in the Chelsea Harbour Club, the Amida is a restful blue oasis. It has all the facilities you need for a wet spa day: a 25-metre lap pool, large jacuzzi, steam room, sauna, ice chute, hydrotherapy pool and heated beds for relaxing. A full range of massages and other treatments are available, and the restaurant serves good fresh food. Look out for special offers and treat yourself to a day of rest and replenishment for body and mind.

amidaspa.co.uk
Harbour Club, Watermeadow Lane
SW6 2RR

AQUILLA AT THE REMBRANDT

In the heart of posh Knightsbridge, the Aquilla Health and Fitness Club is attached to the four-star Rembrandt Hotel, but offers reasonable prices on spa days, especially midweek. There's a swimming pool with a layout reminiscent of an ancient Roman baths, as well as sauna, steam bath, jacuzzi and a limited range of the usual pampering treatments. The restaurant is in the main hotel so you need to be dressed for dining. Look out for special offers on websites like spabreak.com

aquilla.sarova.com
11 Thurloe Place, SW7 2RS

—

SOUNDS AND MUSIC: MINDFUL LISTENING

Sound plays a big part in our experience of city life. Traffic, sirens, car alarms, trains, rubbish lorries, planes overhead, music blaring, workmen shouting, drilling, sawing and clanking. We are tossed and jostled in a sea of sounds until our nerves feel jangled and frayed and we are buzzing with sonic vibrations. We learn to screen much of it out, and sometimes we are surprised by silence when a sound we hadn't even consciously registered suddenly stops.

The experience of quiet can be deeply restorative. It's good to seek out places where we can bathe ourselves in silence, or in natural sounds like birdsong or water. But we can also develop a new relationship with the sounds of the city itself. By making a small but significant mental shift, we can let the sounds be a call to wake us out of autopilot and be present. The act of listening can become a mindful experience which takes us out of our busy thoughts and into this moment. We can also bring this attitude to our experience of music, dropping our mental chatter to enter the flow of sound.

Sound can also be a powerful trigger for opening up to a sense of space. When we are caught up in our internal dialogue, the world can become small and claustrophobic. Suddenly a sound cuts through our awareness – an airplane, a church bell or a car alarm. There's a sense of the sound travelling from a distance, perhaps in the next room, or the next street, or far away - we can open our minds to a vast space which extends in all directions. For a moment the universe is bigger and less centred on 'me'. Mindfulness of sounds can help us nurture this ability to open up to the wider world.

Try this: mindfulness of sounds

You can practise this inside or outdoors. It may be easiest to try it first in a location that is not excessively noisy, but once you get used to it you can practise it anywhere.

- Sit in an upright posture, feeling the weight of your body, your feet on the floor and your bottom on the seat. It may be helpful to close your eyes.

- Now open your awareness to sounds. You may notice sounds far away, nearby, in your own body. You don't need to search for sounds, just let them come to you. Imagine you are a microphone, receiving the sounds without bias.

- Notice the volume, the pitch, the texture. You will probably find yourself labelling the sounds, puzzling about what they are, or creating a storyline around them. There's nothing wrong with this, but when you find yourself caught up in thinking about the sounds, see if you can come back to the direct experience of hearing.

• If your mind wanders, bring it back gently to awareness of sounds. You could also notice the gaps and silences between sounds.

• If there are sounds you dislike, notice if you have any reactions in your body. Are you tightening your stomach or bracing in some way against the sound? See if you can relax and soften by breathing into any parts of the body where there is bracing. Can you make friends with the sounds you find unpleasant, or at least be inquisitive about them? Examine the tone and texture; notice if there are layers of sound, and whether it is continuous or changing. Is it possible to let go of your irritation and struggle with these sounds, and let them be as they are?

• Notice how the sounds are arising and dissolving within a vast space which stretches out in all directions. Sometimes we get caught up in the claustrophobia of our mental chatter. Let the sounds wake you up to this sense of spaciousness.

BIRDSONG

For thousands of years, people have enjoyed the sounds of birds as a connection to the mysterious and magical world of non-human life. The author Aldous Huxley once suggested that if we took birds out of British poetry we would have to drop half of the English canon. In London, even in the most urban landscapes you can usually still hear a bird or two. If we pause for a few moments to listen, the sounds of the birds can cut through our feelings of rush and anxiety for a moment, and open us up to a timeless present.

Birdsong is a strange combination of repetition and unpredictability, with hidden notes and melodies, and subtle intricacies. If you learn to recognise the sounds of particular birds, you'll start to notice them more and appreciate the music of the city's trees and gardens. Each bird has its own distinctive character and call. I'm not a great expert myself, but since doing a little research on the sounds of common London birds I've found that I listen to birdsong in a whole new way, noticing the variety of calls, like human languages.

Try this: listening to birdsong

When you hear a bird, take a few moments to stop and really listen, hearing the tone and texture of the sound. How would you describe it – is it a cawing or cooing, or chirping or cheeping, a trilling or twerping? Close your eyes and notice the gaps between sounds as well – the silences. The birds call through space, inhabiting a vast world which ranges from ground level to the tops of trees and rooftops and the sky above. When you are feeling claustrophobic, let the sound of birds open your mind to a sense of this bigger space.

Familiar London birdsong includes the simple one-note chirp of the house sparrow, the soft cooing of the woodpigeon, and the lyrical bursts of the blackbird. The great tit can sing up to eight songs to trick his rivals into believing that his territory is defended by more birds than just him. Some birds have adapted to city life: the starling is an excellent mimic, and can even copy car alarms. Robins often sing at night because it's quieter, avoiding competition with the high noise levels of city life. You can find audio recordings and images of our most common birds at rspb.org.uk/wildlife/birdguide/. If you become aware that different birds have very different calls, the sounds will become more interesting and alive to you, and you'll find that they naturally wake you up to the freshness of the present moment.

CITY SOUNDS

The way we experience sound is emotionally subjective. For example, if you live near Heathrow airport you might be angered by aircraft noise, but if you work at the airport and depend on it for your livelihood you might hear the sound of planes in a different way. Researchers in New York talked to people having lunch in a small plaza park with a water feature, who said they came there because it was so peaceful. The decibel level of the waterfall was louder than the traffic, but because it was a natural noise people felt calmed by it.

I've had a lifelong dislike of traffic noise, and over the years have found myself being aware of it when others seemed to be oblivious. Once I attended a mindfulness session in a house in Pimlico, with traffic passing continuously outside. I sat there feeling irritated and distracted. Then at some point I noticed my own reaction and how my body was tensing against the sound. I decided to see if I could let go of my negative judgement about it and really listen to the sound. In fact the traffic sound was much more interesting than I thought – not just one sound, but layers and waves of different tones. I realised it had a lot in common with other sounds that I like, such as a waterfall, or waves at the seaside. This transformed my experience and I was able to feel more friendly towards the sounds instead of blocking them out or struggling with them.

Pause: the London siren

The wail of sirens is a constant soundtrack to the city. The London Ambulance Service operates around 900 ambulances, the London Fire Brigade has 155 engines and the Met Police run a fleet of more than 8,000 vehicles. No wonder that in central London we can hear those sirens rising above the urban din every few minutes. Like birdsong, the sirens have different calls – long penetrating wails, shorter oscillating rhythms.

If the piercing sound of a siren cuts through your awareness, instead of letting it irritate you, try thinking of it as a wake-up call. If it feels natural, you might take a moment to think of the injured person and the team rushing to help them, or you could just notice the siren as a sound. You might have been muddling along in a mental fog, caught up in thoughts about the next thing you have to do, or replaying a conversation you had yesterday. At this moment, you are suddenly here and present. Use the sound as a reminder to take a pause, and notice the world around you.

LONDON BELLS

'Oranges and Lemons say the bells of St Clement's ... ' The sound of bells ringing is deeply rooted in London life, and many of the church bells named in the nursery rhyme still ring out today. If you hear bells above the city din as you go about your travels, you could let them be a call to you to stop and listen. Notice their tone and texture – are there words to describe them? 'They were old Chimes, trust me ... ,' wrote Dickens in his story 'The Chimes'; ' ... They had clear, loud, lusty voices, had these Bells, and bent on being heard on stormy nights, by some poor mother watching a sick child.'

Tradition dictates that a true Cockney must be born within earshot of the sound of Bow Bells – that is, the bells of St Mary-le-Bow Church, Cheapside (EC2V 6AU). These bells used to ring out as far as Hackney and Waltham Forest to the north, and down to Southwark across the river, but increased street noise means they can now only be heard within a small area in the City and Shoreditch. If you're close enough to the church, you can hear the Bow Bells strike every 15 minutes, with a toll before daily services and each morning and evening – all done automatically. Change ringing, where each of the 12 bells is rung in a full circle by an individual person, happens on special occasions such as City events or weddings. Bands of experienced ringers come from far and wide to practise on this famous ring of bells. (Visit stmarylebow.co.uk for ringing times.)

Bell-ringing groups are also active right across London with regular change-ringing on Sundays and practice sessions during the week. In the Diocese of London there are over 100 churches and other buildings with bells hung ready for full circle ringing. On a typical Sunday the bells of around 70 per cent of these are rung. If you'd like to seek them out specially, you could have a look on the calendar of the Middlesex County Association & London Diocesan Guild of Church Bell Ringers (mcaldg.org.uk). The Association is keen to train new ringers to ensure the continuance of this ancient art, so contact them if you'd like to learn to ring yourself. Meanwhile, keep an ear out as you travel through the city. Whether it's the simple chiming of the hours or the more complex patterns of bell-ringing, you can pause, be present, and listen to the voice of these bells singing out amidst the more modern sounds of the city.

LISTENING TO MUSIC MINDFULLY

Like any big city, London is filled with music. Tunes and beats of every kind set the mood for socialising, drinking, shopping or clubbing. But as well as being the backdrop for other activities, listening to music in its own right can be one of the most powerful and enjoyable ways of being mindful. When you are really listening, you are here, fully present in the flow of energy and sound.

The American composer Aaron Copland wrote about three ways of listening to music. The 'sensuous plane' is listening for the sheer pleasure of the music, absentmindedly bathing in the sound. It's enjoyable but there is a danger that while in this mode we may drift off into our dreams without listening fully. The 'expressive plane' is where we connect with some kind of deeper meaning in the music, some emotional quality. We notice countless subtle shadings – if there is 'sadness' is it pessimistic or fateful or bittersweet? Often the feelings can't be pinned down in words, but they are no less real. Finally, there is the 'sheerly musical' plane – hearing the melodies, the rhythms, the harmonies and the tone colour;

following the line of the composer's intention. The ideal listener is listening on all three planes at once, and is both inside and outside the music. Copland says we can deepen our understanding of any music by being more conscious and aware, and listening actively.

This has been my own experience, especially with music that I find challenging. I worked for several years for BBC Radio 3, and at one point I found myself filming webcasts for a programme called *Mixing It,* which featured a lot of off-the-wall music: free jazz, electro-acoustic, experimental. I didn't know much about this music, but I listened as intently as I could, and moved the camera from one instrument or voice to another, drawn by the energy of the music. By paying full attention to one musician at a time, and following instinctively as a particular musical line or rhythm took the lead, I found myself enjoying music which was outside my usual comfort zone.

There are probably as many ways of listening as there are listeners, and there is no 'right' way. Daydreaming to music has its place, but if we look at what our minds are doing, we may find that it's not always a very nurturing experience. I know myself, if I drift into my own thoughts, I may get caught up in uselessly replaying conversations or planning tomorrow's schedule, and I find I just missed a beautiful piece of music. If that happens to you, try a more active way of listening. Consciously focus for a while on the rhythm, or an instrument you don't normally listen to, or the emotional quality, or some other element that catches your interest. When you drift away, gently bring yourself back to some aspect of the music, in this moment.

LISTENING AND WORDS

The core practice of mindful listening (as in the exercise on page 143) is about hearing sounds *as sounds*. When we find ourselves caught up in concepts *about* the sounds, we gently return to the direct experience of hearing – the tone, the dynamics, the rhythm and texture. Poetry and spoken word (and music with lyrics) do have this element of pure sound, but they also engage our conceptual minds in making connections and interpreting meanings. This is a different kind of listening, though still requiring an attentiveness which keeps us mindfully present. Poetry has a close relationship to mindfulness: it's often about discovering joy or humour within small moments, and illuminating the magical within the mundane. London has a thriving spoken word scene, with regular readings and open-mic events where you can hear fresh voices every week.

Another type of mindful listening is listening to other people. This is the art of mindful communication; it is a little beyond the scope of this book to explore in detail, but our discourse with others is very much part of city living. So often our communication is rushed – we speak without taking the time to be clear, and we jump in on others as they are speaking without taking the time to listen. Mindful listening here means giving someone our undivided attention – not planning our own speech, but hearing fully what they have to say. As we slow down, we can allow more space so that the other person's meaning unfolds in its own pace. And when we speak ourselves, we might not be so afraid of silence, but can allow pauses to let the right words emerge. Listening becomes an act of trusting the moment, rather than strategising to make everything turn out according to our plans.

MINDFUL GUIDE

Music for listening: venues

UNION CHAPEL

Union Chapel is a magnificent Victorian gothic church in Islington which has become a popular venue for live music. The octagonal chapel was designed by the architect James Cubbitt in 1877 so that 'every person should see and hear the preacher without conscious effort', which has made for excellent acoustics and an intimate atmosphere. The pews are raked so that everyone can clearly see the performers, and the setting is atmospheric with stone arches, stained-glass windows and a domed ceiling. The chapel is host to the annual Little Noise Sessions, which have in the past featured acoustic sets by top artists like Amy Winehouse, Adele, Coldplay, Razorlight and Stereophonics.

unionchapel.org.uk
Compton Avenue, London N1 2XD

CAFÉ OTO

Café Oto is dedicated to showcasing music outside the mainstream, where you can hear interesting and challenging sounds from across the globe. Opened in 2008, it is tucked down an alleyway off Kingsland High Street in Dalston, an area increasingly known for having one of London's liveliest arts scenes. Popular with hipsters and serious music lovers, it's a large open space with minimal décor, where the music is the main attraction. Programming ranges from Japanese underground artists to Norwegian free jazz to new British folk. The bar sells London craft beers, Japanese sake and a wide selection of whiskies. The space runs as a café in the daytime, with live music almost every night of the week.

caféoto.co.uk
18–22 Ashwin Street, E8 3DL

—

KINGS PLACE

This shiny, modern arts venue, which opened in 2008, is at the heart of the redevelopment of the Kings Cross area, just a few minutes' walk from the station. Its two concert halls were the first new public concert halls to be built in London since the Barbican in 1982, designed with excellent acoustics to showcase music of all genres, as well as the spoken word. Kings Place is the permanent home to the London Sinfonietta and the Orchestra of the Age of Enlightenment, and hosts a wide range of jazz, folk and leftfield rock. Concerts are often clustered into festivals and themed weeks curated by musicians. The building also hosts galleries and offices, including the *Guardian* newspaper, and suffers from feeling a little more like an office block than a lively music venue, rather clean and sterile. However, the restaurant and bar have lovely views out over Regent's Canal, with a terrace where you can watch the narrow boats gliding by before or after the concert.

kingsplace.co.uk
90 York Way, N1 9AG

BRUNEL MUSEUM: THAMES TUNNEL

One of London's most unusual venues for music is the Thames Tunnel Shaft, a cavernous underground chamber half the size of Shakespeare's Globe, which musicians describe as 'like performing inside a giant well'. It is part of the Brunel Museum in Rotherhithe, and in the warmer months it plays host to concerts of world and folk music, jazz and Pop-up Opera. The Shaft was originally the entrance to the world's first tunnel under a river, built by the great engineer Isambard Kingdom Brunel and his father, which opened in 1843 as the 'Eighth Wonder of the World'. Recently re-opened, the entrance currently involves stooping through a dark passageway and carefully descending via steep makeshift stairs, although a more accessible entryway is planned. It's a magical place for a gig, with its other-worldly atmosphere and the acoustics of an underground cathedral. Look out also for events in the garden above the Thames

Tunnel, which is transformed into a pop-up cocktail bar during the summer season.

brunel-museum.org.uk
Railway Avenue, SE16 4LF

—

WIGMORE HALL

One of the world's top chamber music venues, the Wigmore Hall has superb acoustics and beautiful art nouveau décor. It hosts around 400 events a year, including Monday lunchtime concerts, which are broadcast on BBC Radio 3, and Sunday morning concerts – both with affordable ticket prices. It was built in 1901 and originally named Bechstein Hall, for the German piano maker whose London showroom was next door. Above the stage, the dramatic arts and crafts cupola is decorated with an allegorical painting by F. Lynne Jenkins which represents 'mankind's struggle to catch an echo of the music of the gods'. It's the place to hear the world's top soloists and ensembles of the classical music scene, as well as the best up-and-coming artists.

wigmore-hall.org.uk
36 Wigmore Street, W1U 2BP

—

SOUTHBANK CENTRE

Every Londoner knows the Southbank, one of the world's largest arts centres with its iconic concert halls and mind-boggling programme of events. However, not everyone knows – or remembers – that its public spaces are alive with music and performance every day of the week and that these are absolutely free. Pop in during lunchtimes and early evenings on a weekday, or almost any time on the weekend, and you are likely to hear something interesting in one of the foyers, often linked to one of the Southbank's many themed seasons and festivals. The Royal Festival Hall can be a particularly relaxing place to hang out, with a sense of vast indoor space which can absorb a lot of people before it feels overcrowded. You can pick up a coffee at EAT or a drink from the bar, but you can also sit all day without buying anything. You can find a table or sofa in various nooks and crannies near the music, or near the riverside when things are quiet.

southbankcentre.co.uk
Belvedere Road, SE1 8XX

—

THE BEDFORD

This Balham pub has made a name for itself on the acoustic scene, with free live music showcases every Monday to Thursday, 50 weeks of the year. Artists such as James Morrison, KT Tunstall and Ed Sheeran played here before they were big, and others like Pete Townshend and Willy Mason have played secret or impromptu shows here. Gigs take place in the upstairs room known as the 'Globe Theatre', and audiences are expected to listen rather than chat when the artists are playing. With its mission to discover and promote emerging acts, the Bedford Live has

taken showcases to festivals around the UK and in the States, and holds its own festivals within the venue such as the London FolkFest.

thebedford.co.uk
77 Bedford Hill, SW12 9HD

—

Music for listening: festivals and events

MELTDOWN

Every June the Southbank Centre is host to Meltdown, a music and arts festival curated by some of the world's most iconic and innovative musicians. Since the event began in 1993, curators have included David Bowie, Patti Smith, Yoko Ono, Elvis Costello, Jarvis Cocker and Massive Attack – each putting their own spin on the festival. As well as top bands the festival includes film, exhibitions, performance art and genre-defying collaborations.

meltdown.southbankcentre.co.uk
South Bank Centre, Belvedere Road, SE1 8XX

LONDON JAZZ FESTIVAL

In the darkening month of November, the London Jazz Festival takes over London for the city's biggest pan-city music festival, encompassing large concert halls like the Barbican and the Royal Festival Hall, and many smaller venues like Ronnie Scott's, The Vortex, the Electric Ballroom and Green Note. Jazz here is a broad church, embracing traditions from across the globe and influences from funk, dubstep, folk, soul, ska, R&B and every other genre. The festival's mission to take jazz to all four corners of the city means that it's worth looking out for free concerts in public spaces.

londonjazzfestival.org.uk

—

THE PROMS

The famous BBC Proms is an 8-week summer season of daily concerts in the majestic setting of the Royal Albert Hall. It features mainly orchestral classical music, with smatterings of jazz, world music, gospel and choral; as well as chamber music in the more intimate setting of the Cadogan Hall. The Proms have been a London institution since 1895, when musical impressario Robert Newman came up with the idea of an indoor version of the promenade concerts which had long been popular in London's pleasure gardens. With low ticket prices and an informal atmosphere, his intention was to 'train the public' to attend classical music concerts. The tradition of 'Promming' means that for only £5 you can buy a ticket on the day for the standing areas in the hall. Plonk yourself directly in front of the orchestra and immerse yourself in sound, or high up in the gallery for a different experience of the music wafting up through the space.

bbc.co.uk/proms
Royal Albert Hall, Kensington Gore, SW7 2AP

—

SOMERSET HOUSE SUMMER SERIES

Over recent years, many of London's most beautiful historic buildings and parks have been developed as summer concert backdrops. Kenwood House in Hampstead was one of the first to do this, with its outdoor concerts becoming a highlight of London summers from 1951 onwards. Kew Gardens has its 'Kew the Music' festival, and there's a Hampton Court Palace Festival in its Tudor setting. The beautiful neo-classical courtyard of Somerset House hosts a summer concert series each July, with past artists including Lily Allen, Adele, Basement Jaxx, Goldfrapp, Orbital, PJ Harvey and Of Monsters and Men. With lights dramatically illuminating the opulent 18th-century buildings, and a breeze from the open sky, this is an inspiring place to listen to some of the pop world's big headliners.

somersethouse.org.uk/music
Somerset House, Strand, WC2R 1LA

—

FIELD DAY

The festival of choice for East London hipsters, Field Day takes over Victoria Park in the summer for an outdoor feast of alternative music. Acts range from indie rock to melancholy folk to underground dance to Afro-beat, with headliners such as Metronomy, Pixies and Franz Ferdinand. The one-day event has been held on various dates between May to August, with the festival expanding in 2014 to a whole weekend in June. Expect queues and crowds, but if you're okay with the usual summer-festival inconveniences, it's a chance to treat your ears to a fresh, eclectic mix of music in the setting of a leafy green London park.

fielddayfestivals.com
Victoria Park, Grove Road, E3

—

Poetry and spoken word

APPLES AND SNAKES

Apples and Snakes has been at the forefront of performance poetry and spoken word in the UK for over 30 years. On their website you'll find events happening in London every week, from pubs to major theatres, and from open-mic nights to established headline acts.

applesandsnakes.org

—

POETRY CAFÉ

This Covent Garden café holds poetry readings almost every night, with regular events taking place weekly or monthly. The Tuesday night open-mic session, Poetry Unplugged, offers a chance for poets to read in public for the first time, while other nights feature exiled poets, female writers or curated evenings which mix poetry and music. During the day the café is a relaxed place for coffee and tea and vegetarian lunches.

poetrysociety.org.uk/content/cafe/
22 Betterton Street, WC2H 9BX

—

HAMMER AND TONGUE

Hammer and Tongue is a national network of poetry slams, committed to launching the careers of new poets and touring established names. Their monthly poetry slams in Hackney attract the 'hip hop generation' to the old-fashioned, low-tech medium of poetry.

hammerandtongue.com

—

MINDFUL
EATING

In the first week of my mindfulness courses, one piece of homework I set for participants is to eat a meal mindfully. The idea is to choose one meal during the week where they pay full attention to the experience of eating, rather than distracting themselves with other things. Usually quite a few people will come back saying they found this really difficult: it made them uncomfortable or bored, they worried they would 'go off' their food, or they did go off their food, or they just felt inexplicably fearful. Many of us are so used to multi-tasking when we eat, or entertaining ourselves with TV and radio, that this simple act is no longer a source of enjoyment in its own right.

Mindful eating is about bringing back that enjoyment of tasting and savouring what we put in our mouths. Eating mindfully, we are able to appreciate one of life's greatest and most basic pleasures. We also eat the right amount because we notice when we are full instead of wolfing things down. We drink more slowly instead of knocking it back and getting drunk too fast. We may also naturally eat more healthily by paying attention to what we are eating instead of absent-mindedly shovelling in a packet of crisps without really tasting them.

When I first started work at the BBC we used to take proper lunches, going out to the local Italian for a hot meal, or in summer for a picnic on the lawn of a nearby square. Now in many of London's workplaces it's more common to eat *al desko* than *al fresco* – consuming a sandwich at our desk while surfing the web, and getting to the end of lunch having hardly tasted a bite. Fast food has its place, and many of us only manage to juggle the demands of city life by relying some of the time on convenience food – I've found myself that working parenthood is often workable thanks to quick-cook ravioli and ready-made soup. For me, mindful eating is less about being too fanatical about the food itself being haute cuisine, and more about appreciating whatever it is that we are eating.

Try this: mindful eating

- Fetch yourself a couple of pieces of dried or fresh fruit: the classic choice is raisins but you could use grapes, satsuma segments or any other small piece of food.

- Take the raisin or fruit in your palm. Imagine you've never seen it before. Pick it up and take a good look at its shape, colour, texture, folds and hollows, the light and shade. Take time to explore it with your eyes.

- Investigate the raisin or fruit with your other senses. What does it feel like between your fingers? Does it make a sound if you squish it near your ear? Notice what it smells like, and if you have any reaction to its aroma.

- Whenever your mind wanders off, notice this happening and be aware of any thoughts that arise.

- Bring the food to your mouth, first running it along the lips, noticing any reactions – maybe saliva in the mouth. Place it in your mouth, without chewing yet. Explore any textures and flavours that are here before you bite. Finally, take a bite into it, noticing the taste and texture as you chew.

- Then swallow it – see if you can follow it as it moves downwards. Are there any after-effects – after-taste, or feelings, or thoughts?

- Now you can take a second raisin or piece of fruit and go through the exercise again. Is it the same experience as the first time? Slowly explore it with each of your senses, and notice if the experience is the same or different from the first time.

Most of us don't often pay this much attention when we're eating – we'll shovel in a handful of raisins, or eat them absent-mindedly in a bowl of muesli. You might find that it was hard to keep your mind on the exercise, or you felt irritated, wanting to go faster. We don't have to eat all of our food at a snail's pace, but by slowing down a little and paying attention, the experience can become more vivid and satisfying. We can experience the flavour and texture of the small moments that make up our lives – the little raisins which we so often miss. Sometimes people report that when they eat mindfully they discover they don't need as big a portion as they thought – they were shovelling it in without noticing when their body was satisfied. Or it could be the opposite, that you forget to eat properly, and that being more mindful helps you make sure to get enough nourishment.

SLOW FOOD

The Slow Food movement celebrates slowing down, knowing where our food comes from and promoting local producers and sustainable farming practices. The movement was born in Italy in the 1980s as a reaction to the arrival of a McDonald's franchise in a historic piazza in Rome. It is a now a global, grassroots movement with thousands of members, including a programme of events and markets in London (slowfood.org.uk/ slowfoodlondon.com).

Slow Food puts a lot of emphasis on the origin and production of food, and this is of course important, both for ourselves and the planet. However, it's good also to bring this 'slow' approach into the act of eating itself. Food is a popular subject in the media, with bake-offs and celebrity chefs getting high ratings. But sometimes it seems we fetishise the cooking and preparing of food while somehow being unable to enjoy the end product. Eating a nice crisp apple can be as rich an experience as consuming a complicated meal, if we take time to notice its textures and flavours. When we slow down and pay attention, it can also naturally make us a bit more mindful of what we're eating and where it came from, which can only be good for our own physical health as well as the ethics of the food chain.

Cooking itself can, of course, be a wonderful opportunity for mindfulness. We can rush through the task, resenting every moment, or we can slow down and enjoy the activity of preparing the food. When you find your mind is miles away, perhaps re-running your day or worrying about tomorrow, try bringing your full attention to the weight and texture of a potato in your hand, and the act of washing and peeling. You could notice each ingredient as you prepare it – its shape, its colour, the miraculous fact that this produce has arrived in your kitchen from a farm somewhere, and is now here for you to eat. After a day at the computer or in meetings, there can be something hugely therapeutic about the tactile sensations of chopping vegetables or stirring a casserole. You can let these seemingly routine activities be a way to come out of your busy head and back into your body, and into the physical world of carrots and potatoes and parsley.

HOME GROWN

With our supermarket aisles offering us green beans from Kenya and strawberries from Spain, recent decades have seen a growing movement to reduce our food miles and support local produce. Farmers' markets have been popping up on Saturdays and Sundays in car parks and school playgrounds around the city, selling seasonal fruit and veg, pies and sausages, cheeses, artisan bread and many more delights. The umbrella organisation, London Farmers' Markets, has strict rules that the foods on sale must be produced within 100 miles of the M25, and sold only by the producers themselves.

While farm produce like fruit and veg is of course mainly grown outside London itself, there's a product that is having a revival within the city: the craft beer. There are now more than 30 independent breweries within the magic circle of the M25, offering home-grown alternatives to mass-produced commercial beers. Craft beer is a younger cousin of Real Ale, which can tend towards a beard-and-sandals image (not always appealing to Londoners) and has strict rules on production methods. The Craft Beer movement is relaxed about how the beer is made, as long as it is brewed for taste rather than volume.

Independent breweries in London include The Camden Town Brewery, with its pale 'Hell's Lager', and Sambrook Brewery in Battersea, which makes 'Wandle Ale' near south London's River Wandle. The Kernal in Rotherhithe has a flagship stout made to a 19th-century recipe; and the Beavertown Brewery in Hackney features 'Smog Rocket' porter. When we drink the usual big-name beers, it can be easy to go into autopilot, knocking back the familiar liquid without really noticing much about its taste. Craft beer is bursting with unusual and experimental flavours, so like it or not, it encourages us to taste it fully as it's going down.

COFFEE AND TEA

Coffee is a mixed blessing when it comes to mindfulness. On the one hand, it can offer us the excuse we need to take a break, to stretch our legs walking to the kettle or to the coffee shop, and to enjoy some quiet moments sitting and sipping. On the other hand, when our day includes too many hits of caffeine we enter a jittery adrenaline buzz which keeps us in fast-forward mode, unable to settle into the present. If we drink our coffee mindfully, we can enjoy its taste, notice its effects and realise when it might be time to ask for decaffeinated, or to switch to another drink.

Like alcohol, many of us tend to use coffee to self-medicate against the stresses of city life. When we're feeling flat, tired or strung out, we escape the present by looking for that artificial lift. It can help to stock the cupboard and fridge with some enticing alternatives.

I've recently been experimenting with teas – caffeine-free ones like rooibos or exotic fruit mixes – which I can brew up instead of that extra cup of caffeine, or glass of wine in the evening. Instead of feeding my coffee buzziness – or alcoholic fuzziness – I finish the drink feeling more rested, healthy and present.

Try this: a tea break

Throughout the day we can use very simple activities as a way of slowing down, creating a gap and taking a few minutes to be present. The traditional cup of tea is something many of us use as a natural break in offices and homes across London, but often even this can be done in a rush: at the first sip our head is already in our next task. You can turn the tea break into a more nurturing experience by bringing mindfulness into the act of making and drinking tea.

- Bring awareness to your body sensations as you make the tea. Feel the weight of the kettle and your actions as you fill it with water and set it to boil.

- While the water is boiling, bring your attention to the contact of your feet on the floor. Notice that you are breathing, bringing awareness to the movement of your breath wherever you feel it in the body. Rest your mind on this soothing rhythm of the breath.

- Make the tea with your full attention on what you are doing: choosing the cup, placing the tea or teabag in the pot or cup, pouring in the water, and so on. If you are waiting for it to steep, you could again bring awareness to your breath while you wait.

- When the tea is made, drink it mindfully, enjoying the warmth of the cup, the smell, the taste and heat of the tea. If you have to take it to your desk or continue with your next task, see if you can drink at least part of your cup with full attention and appreciation.

- Try to make space for pauses like this as often as you can, creating gaps within your busyness and discursiveness. In this way you can nurture and enjoy the simple moments which make up the flow of life.

MINDFUL CAFÉS AND PUBS

With thousands of cafés and restaurants in London, you can find inspiring food from virtually every cultural background in every borough. So what makes for a mindful London meal? One element is the food itself: something healthy and flavoursome, so when we slow down and pay attention, we still feel good about putting it into our body. The other is the environment – does it feed our freneticism, or does it support us to appreciate our food and the whole experience of eating?

In the Guide I mention a few cafés that feel like mindful places to me, but the main thing is to seek out your own in your neighbourhood. If at lunch you tend to dash out and bring back a sandwich to your desk, can you allow yourself ten more minutes to sit down at your local café? There is something luxurious about sitting alone at a table, enjoying each bite without multi-tasking, and watching the other customers or the world rushing by outside. We may think we can't spare a moment, but by creating this small gap we are shifting our relationship to time. By slowing down and being present for a few minutes, we are saying to ourselves that this moment, today, is important, not just all the plans we are working on for tomorrow and next week and next year. We nourish ourselves in this moment, and as a by-product it's quite likely we will be more productive when we return to our tasks and plans.

The pub can be another wonderful place to take time out on your own, especially when you stumble across an old-fashioned wood-panelled haven, without music or a TV blaring – perhaps with some comfortable nooks and crannies, or a fireplace, or a garden terrace. Sitting alone in the pub is again a statement to yourself that you are comfortable in your own skin, able to be here without being entertained in every moment. Try sipping your coffee or drink without checking your emails or scanning the newspaper – if you feel self-conscious you can put your paper or mobile on the table as a prop. No one else will know you are sitting here doing nothing – or almost nothing – just enjoying the taste of your drink, the babble of conversation, and the view of the pub and its clientele.

MINDFUL GUIDE

Food markets

WHITECROSS STREET MARKET

Popular with workers in Clerkenwell and Old Street, Whitecross Street swells on Thursdays and Fridays into a specialist food market with up to 50 stalls and vans. Whitecross Street is one of the oldest markets in London, having operated for over 150 years. Stallholders sell street food for reasonable prices: you can savour the different flavours and textures of Greek, Turkish, Italian, Indian, Thai and Mexican dishes. For British specialties, 'Eat my Pies' is popular, offering pork pies, Scotch eggs and custard tarts. While the food is global, the experience is local, often cooked in front of you, so you feel more closely connected to the provenance than when buying a sandwich from a big chain. Some of the stalls pack up after lunch, so try and arrive by 2pm.

Whitecross Street, EC1Y 8QJ

REAL FOOD MARKET, SOUTHBANK CENTRE

What used to be a boring concrete square at the back of the Royal Festival Hall is now a riot of colours and smells every Friday to Sunday. Rows of cheerful green and white marquees are host to street food vendors and small food producers. You can follow your nose to huge pans of steaming paella, sweet crêpes or a Korean barbeque. Or to take home there are Ethiopian coffee beans, French macaroons, Somerset cheeses and Italian gnocchi. Although it can get busy, there is generally a festive atmosphere, relaxed and cheerful. These markets are run by Real Food Festivals whose aim is 'to reconnect people back to where their food comes from and to promote the idea of buying directly from the people who actually produce our food.'

realfoodfestival.co.uk
Southbank Centre Square,
Belvedere Road, SE1 8XX

LONDON FARMERS' MARKETS

London Farmers' Markets runs about 20 markets across London, with strict rules: only produce from within 100 miles of the M25, and no middlemen, so you are buying direct from the farmer, fisherman or baker. Brixton Station Road fills up every Sunday morning with fruit and veg stalls, organic meats, and Caribbean vegan pastries. Marylebone market, also Sunday morning, is a foodie destination with producers selling exotic mushrooms, Kent goat's cheese and Hertfordshire honey. Markets operate from Ealing and Twickenham in the west to Walthamstow and Blackheath in the east, each with their regular stallholders.

lfm.org.uk
See web for times and locations

—

Tea shops

POSTCARD TEAS

Tempt yourself away from the coffee buzz with a soothing cup of exotic tea. This Mayfair shop is a place of pilgrimage for serious tea lovers, with shelves of beautifully packaged caddies of teas from across Asia. The company claims to be the first in the world to put the maker's name and location on all its teas, including the blends. Postcard sells tea from small farms of less than 15 acres, where it says the very best teas are grown. The team are English, Chinese and Japanese and work closely with the small growers they promote. Here you can find rare and precious teas such as 'Master Xu's Fragment of Imperial Red Robe' and 'Lotus Lake Green'. There are also many more common teas such as Darjeelings, Lapsangs, Oolongs, Jasmines and English Breakfast blends.

postcardteas.com
Dering Street, W1S 1AG

—

CAFÉ GOSSIP

Café Gossip is a small, welcoming tea shop stocked with an amazing range of teas and staffed by tea-lovers happy to chat you through the varieties. At the back of the shop is a peaceful place to sit drinking the tea and eating cake while immersed in the aromas of flowers and spices. Buy a packet or two to bring home: ranging from green teas to Rooibos Chai, to fruity mixes with pungent ingredients like elderberries, hibiscus and beetroot.

62 Broadway Market, E8 4QJ

—

THE TEA HOUSE

This family-run business opened in Covent Garden in 1982, selling a wide range of black, red, oolong, pu-erh, green and white teas and herbal infusions. The shop glows red and black like a Japanese lacquer tea set, chock full of tea packets and canisters, teapots and teacups, and other tea paraphernalia. The Tea House

is known by connoisseurs for its selection of green and white teas, which are low in caffeine and celebrated for their health properties. There's also an inviting selection of fruit and flower infusions such as Turkish Apple, Morocco Orange, Pure Rosebuds and Camomile and Lemongrass. They sell black teas for the traditional British palate, and a range of flavoured black teas such as Apricot, Crème Caramel and Very Spicy Chai.

theteahouseltd.com
15 Neal Street, WC2H 9PU

—

Cafés

FEDERATION COFFEE

Brixton Village Market has been through an astounding transformation in recent years, from run-down units with 50 per cent occupancy to a thriving destination for foodies. Federation Coffee has been here since the revival began, on a corner site with tables outside under the vaulted 1920s arcade. They roast their own coffee locally with beans from Brazil, Ethiopia, El Salvador and Sumatra, and also serve pastries, cakes and savouries. It's a small place with only a few tables, so not easy to get one at peak times – go in quieter daytime hours if you can for a place to sit, open your senses and watch the world go by.

federationcoffee.com
Unit 77–78, Brixton Village Market, SW9 8PS

—

THE COUNTER CAFÉ

This much-loved Hackney café sits right next to the River Lea, amidst warehouses and artists' studios, with the Olympic Stadium looming across the river. It shares a building with Stour Space gallery, with the café at the back. The décor is rough and ready, with exposed brick, bare floors and rows of old cinema chairs. Popular dishes include Eggs Benedict, handmade pies and bacon sandwiches. There are big windows

both upstairs and downstairs for views out over the canal, or in good weather you can sit out on the terrace made of floating pontoons, and enjoy the post-industrial riverside landscape.

thecountercafé.co.uk
7 Roach Road, E3 2PA

—

RIBA RESTAURANT

A peaceful haven within the grandeur of the Royal Institute of British Architects, which is a stunning example of early 1930s Art Deco architecture. The old restaurant location in Florence Hall is now used for private events, so the restaurant is housed in the former first-floor gallery. Walk up the grand marble stairwell to reach this simple, bright room with floor-to-ceiling windows looking out over Portland Place. It's a good place to escape the crowds of Oxford Circus for a morning coffee, bistro-style lunch or afternoon tea. While you're there, you could have a look at one of RIBA's regular free exhibitions in the gallery spaces, on architectural themes past and present.

architecture.com
66 Portland Place, WIB IAD

—

WILD FOOD CAFÉ

When it feels like a moment to eat something exceptionally healthy, the Wild Food Café has the menu. It serves vegan and vegetarian food with an emphasis on raw foods, wild foods, 'superfoods' and organic produce. Dishes include shiitake, raw olive and dulse burgers; hummus with beetroot and carrot salad; or sheep's cheese on sourdough bread. To drink, there are organic juices and smoothies such as 'Incredible Green', which includes kale, celery and fresh Irish moss. The café is founded on a passionate belief that these raw and healthy foods are the key to vitality, and to changing the planet. There's a big open kitchen with a counter around it and shared tables, which can get busy, so it's not the place for solitude, but certainly a place where

you can pay full attention to the food and feel happy with what you are putting in your body. It's located in colourful Neal's Yard, long-time home to various healthy shops and cafés, clustered together in a courtyard near Covent Garden.

wildfoodcafé.com
Ist Floor, 14 Neal's Yard, WC2H 9DP

—

CAFÉ IN THE CRYPT

The 18th-century crypt under St Martin-in-the-Fields is enormous and cavernous, but it swallows up the crowds of Londoners and tourists, enveloping all in a sense of peace and quiet. The food is served caféteria-style: the simple British fare you might find in museum cafés and stately homes, including soups, salads, sandwiches, hot dishes, puddings and cakes. There's a restful, timeless quality as you sit under brick-vaulted ceilings with soft yellow lighting and tombstones underfoot. A good place to eat a reasonable meal that is quick without feeling rushed, or to recuperate with a hot drink just a stone's throw from Charing Cross, the Strand and the West End. On Wednesday evenings there are jazz nights with live bands.

stmartin-in-the-fields.org/café-in-the-crypt
St Martin-in-the-Fields, Trafalgar Square, WC2N 4JJ

—

Pubs

CRAFT BEER COMPANY

Launched in 2011, this small but growing chain has five London pubs in Clerkenwell, Islington, Brixton, Clapham and Covent Garden. They all serve at least 30 draft beers and hundreds of bottled beers. The beers are curated by enthusiastic staff, who will help you select from cask ales made by UK independent micro-breweries, imported small batch keg beer, and bottles from around the globe – or from a range of wines, bourbons, gins, vodkas, and so on. The Islington branch

has a particularly comfortable atmosphere, with old-world décor and a small garden. The Clapham branch is away from the busy high road, and you'll find no TV screens, but instead board games like Scrabble, and a heated beer garden. A place to slow down and appreciate what you are drinking.

thecraftbeerco.com

—

THE MAYFLOWER

There are many historic pubs along the Thames Path, all of which pack out on warm evenings, but if you can come on a quiet weekday there's nothing more relaxing than sitting with a drink by the riverside. The Mayflower claims to be the oldest pub on the River Thames, standing near the moorings from which the pilgrims set sail in 1620. The current pub dates from the 18th century, with comfortable nooks and crannies, oak beams and wooden panelling. There's an upstairs dining room looking out on the water, although the food is a little pricey. The deck has a heated outdoor marquee area with views up towards London Bridge and The Shard, and across to the wharves of Shadwell and Wapping.

themayflowerrotherhithe.com
117 Rotherhithe Street, SE16 4NF

—

THE SPANIARDS INN

The garden of this old London favourite is enormous, with seating for over 400, shady nooks and beautiful mature trees. It's like a country pub in the city, all wood-panelled inside with fires in the winter. The Spaniards Inn is a 16th-century coaching inn with an illustrious history: it features in Dickens' *The Pickwick Papers* and was a haunt of Byron, Keats, Karl Marx and Bram Stoker. Food is pub classics like fish and chips, sausage and mash, seasonal pies and a few gastro dishes. A good place to come after a walk on the nearby Hampstead Heath or the grounds of Kenwood House.

thespaniardshampstead.co.uk
Spaniards Road, NW3 7JJ

—

YE OLDE MITRE

One of London's most atmospheric historic pubs, Ye Olde Mitre was built in 1546 for the servants of the Bishop of Ely. It is hidden down an alleyway, which turns into a courtyard drinking space in good weather. Inside are several quirky, intimate drinking spaces, with thick glass tavern windows, wood panels and old furniture. There are real ales on tap, scrumpy cider and a snack menu. It's a small pub which gets overrun during lunch hours and after work, so for a quieter experience come for a morning or mid-afternoon break. Combine it with a trip to nearby St Etheldreda's, Britain's oldest Catholic church (see Chapter 5).

yeoldemitreholborn.co.uk
1 Ely Place, EC1N 6SJ

—

THE HEIGHTS

The Heights offers one of the best views of central London, where you can spend quiet time reflecting on the beauty of the city and the vastness of the skyline. Just north of Oxford Circus, next to BBC Broadcasting House, is a very unpromising-looking building called the St George's Hotel. It looks like a bland, concrete hotel, of the kind many of us would avoid unless stuck with a delay at an airport. However, enter the lobby and take the lift up 15 floors to the top floor and you'll find a restaurant and bar. Sometimes the space is booked for private events, but usually during the daytime you can sit over a leisurely coffee or glass of wine, relaxing in comfortable leather chairs in the Lounge. Big ceiling-to-floor windows look out over the spire of All Souls, Langham Place, the only surviving church by Regency architect John Nash, and over the rooftops beyond. Here you can re-connect a sense of space and perspective.

saintgeorgeshotel.com/the-heights-restaurant-and-bar

14–15 Langham Place, Regent Street, W1B 2QS

—

MINDFUL MOVEMENT

Living in a big city like London, we may spend a lot of the time feeling disembodied. We sit at our computers staring at screens, with all our activity happening from the neck up. We pump in caffeine and forget to eat, or stretch, or get fresh air. Then after work we may go running or to the gym, where we try to exert our control over the body – no pain, no gain. We behave as if our mind is the boss and the body is a big dumb friend, which we don't even treat in a friendly way.

Mindfulness helps us to bring the mind and body into synch, to be embodied. We can do this in stillness with sitting meditation practices, or in movement. In fact, many people find that movement is one of the most natural ways to connect with the experience of mindfulness, and if you're an adrenaline junkie who finds it hard to sit still, movement may be a good starting place. It's helpful to choose a tradition which has been deliberately created to be a mindfulness practice, like yoga or tai chi, but you can also bring mindfulness into any kind of physical exercise or sport. Ultimately, all movement becomes an opportunity to be mindful. Our bodies are naturally moving as we go about our day, and we can bring our awareness to the sensations of the body in motion at any moment.

Try this: mindful movement

Here is a short, simple stretch to give you the idea of mindful movement. The main point is to be fully inside your body, bringing awareness to the sensations in each moment and being curious about exactly what you feel. Explore your own 'edge' of comfort: what tells you when you are pushing too much, or when you could stretch yourself a bit further? Listen to your own body and only do what is right for you.

- **Standing**: Feel the contact of your feet on the floor – the toes, balls and heels of both feet. Bend the knees a little, and breathe. Feel the crown of your head reaching upwards, and your shoulders relaxing. Have a sense of the space around you. Notice how your body is feeling in this moment – tired, energised, relaxed, tense. Don't try to change it, just notice.

- **Arm stretches**: Turn your palms out and slowly raise your arms away from your sides and upwards towards the sky. Notice where you feel sensations as you move. When you reach the top, keep the shoulders relaxed, and stretch up through the fingertips. Play with your 'edge' – can you stretch more or do you need to ease off, and what exactly is telling you this? When you're ready, lower the arms, again noticing sensations. When your arms reach your sides, stand and breathe, noticing any after-effects of the movement. Repeat a few times, breathing in as you raise the arms, and exhaling as you lower them.

- **Side stretches**: Once again, raise your arms towards the sky and stay there. Tilt from your waist to the left, reaching your arms up and over to the left so that you feel a stretch in the right side of your body. Again, explore how far to stretch without straining, and notice what tells you this – can you listen to your body rather than your mind? If there are intense sensations, try breathing into the area where you can feel them and see if you can soften rather than bracing and clenching. Come back to centre and stretch to the other side, again exploring your 'edge'. Return to centre and lower the arms. Come back to stillness and take a few moments to notice any effects of the movement, and the sense of being present in the body.

See if you can bring some of this awareness of body sensations into your physical activities and your daily life.

SLOW MOTION

Mindful movement doesn't have to be slow, but slower movements give us a chance to feel our body sensations fully. Instead of trying to keep up and get things right, by slowing down we have time to be present with what's happening in each moment. Some physical traditions like yoga, Tai Chi and Qigong were especially developed as forms of moving meditation, with the aim of focusing the energies of the body and the mind. London is rich with groups and centres teaching these practices, and you can find a class in virtually every corner of the city.

Yoga comes in many forms; some may be more conducive to mindfulness than others. The original purpose of yoga, according to Patanjali who wrote the first description of the classical yoga tradition some 2,000 years ago, was to 'still the fluctuations of the mind', or we could say, to quiet down our mental chatter. If the atmosphere of your class is more about looking good on the yoga mat or pushing the body beyond its limits, you may not be in the best place to practise mindfully. If you're new to yoga, look for a class that says 'beginners' or 'introductory' or 'gentle' – this will give you the time to explore the postures with awareness of what effects they are having. You can always head for more demanding classes once you've got the basics.

Pilates has a shorter history than yoga, having been created in the early 20th century by the German-born Joseph Pilates as an exercise system for strengthening the body and restoring structural imbalances. Pilates practice can be an opportunity for mindful movement, focusing on feeling the sensations of the body: on breathing, alignment, using the right muscles and relaxing the ones that are not being used. Like yoga, you will get the most from it by learning the exercises slowly and carefully, establishing the technique rather than rushing through it.

Tai Chi and Qigong were developed in China, and like yoga they work with synchronising body and mind and cultivating internal energy – called 'chi'. Tai Chi has mindfulness at its core, asking the practitioner to be fully present in body and mind in each moment. The slow, gentle movements and deep breathing encourage awareness, as well as increasing health and vitality. Qigong or Chi Kung translates as 'energy work' and is made up of exercises for stretching and mobilising the body and joints, breathing practices, slow movement exercises, standing postures, walking exercises and meditation.

As with yoga, almost every London neighbourhood has Tai Chi and Qigong classes, which are often held in church halls, schools and gyms rather than dedicated centres. And as in China, you can also find classes outdoors in some of our parks, from Twickenham to Hampstead Heath to Walthamstow – do a web search for 'Tai Chi London parks' to find the latest details.

SWIMMING AND RUNNING: MONOTONOUS OR MINDFUL?

Swimming is one of the best forms of exercise, but I have often heard people say they find it boring. Maybe it's because, unlike when you go to the gym or take a run, you can't watch a screen or immerse yourself in pumping music. With swimming it's just back and forth, length after length, with nothing but the breath and the body as entertainment. But with a bit of a mental shift, this very repetitiveness can be soothing and can become a blessing rather than a trial. What happens if you pay attention to each stroke – the sensations in the arms, the kick of the legs, the feeling of your breath, the gliding motion through water, the firmness of the wall as you turn? Each time your mind drifts off into thoughts, you gently bring it back into your body. If you normally count lengths, try swimming for an overall length of time instead, so you can relax into the experience rather than filling your head with numbers. The act of swimming becomes an opportunity to bathe the mind, as well as the body, in cool water.

'Wild swimming' or outdoor swimming promotes the joy of swimming under an open sky. So you can join the pleasures of mindful movement with the freshness and spaciousness of nature.

The manifesto of the Outdoor Swimming Society proclaims: 'Water needs no roof! We believe swimmers have too long been held in chlorinated captivity! Everyone with a set of bathers should be set free to immerse themselves in nature.' There are a number of wild swimming locations in London, including ponds, reservoirs, and freshwater outdoor pools. An online 'wild swim map' at wildswim. com will help you find a location near you.

Like swimming, running is another activity where the repetitive quality can become a meditation rather than a trial. Often our approach may be to run despite the messages of the body, pushing through any pain and driving ourselves too hard too soon. We might use music to block out our present experience and environment. Mindful running is an alternative approach, based on being present in the body, and in this moment, which can help to improve your form, reduce injury and increase the sheer joy of running and being alive.

The movement for barefoot running seems to be very much in tune with this mindful approach. Also known as 'natural running', it is simply running in bare feet or in specialised, minimal, thin-soled shoes. Barefoot runners say the biomechanics are more natural as the forefoot or mid-foot strikes the ground, reducing the risk of chronic injuries caused by the impact of heel striking in padded shoes. More crucially for mindfulness, they say that barefoot running encourages you to slow down and focus on your form, and on the feedback you get from the terrain, rather than achieving long distances beyond your limits. The experience is more relaxing, less goal-oriented, and more about enjoying the journey.

Try this: mindful running

♦ Start slowly, walking and feeling the contact of your feet on the earth. (See mindful walking in Chapter 3.)

♦ As you begin to run, bring awareness to your immediate physical experience: your breath, the way your body moves, your feet striking the earth, and your senses. Don't focus in too hard on one element, or you might forget to watch out for traffic and puddles and fallen branches. Instead, relax into the experience of running.

♦ When the mind drifts off somewhere else, simply bring yourself back to the feeling of your body and the air moving in and out of your lungs.

DANCING

One form of movement practised by thousands of Londoners each week is not something we think of as a sport, but dancing for a few hours can feel as good as any workout. Dancing can be one of the most enjoyable experiences of being in the body – creative, energising and exhilarating. It's a natural place to play with the experience of different paces, as every DJ knows when they hit on the perfect rhythm and beats for the crowd.

London can offer a great night out in a club or bar, but there can be other priorities and challenges which get in the way of enjoying the dancing for its own sake, such as flirting with a partner, looking good on the dance floor, finding enough space, or the opposite

– no one else dancing when you're itching to move. For dancing stripped back to basics, the Five Rhythms movement takes it out of the clubs and into church halls and dance studios around the city. In each session, the music progresses through five rhythms which encourage different ways of moving: flowing, staccato, chaos, lyrical and stillness. This might not be for you if you need three pints and your favourite familiar tunes before you feel ready to move, but for the less self-conscious, this can be a chance to really explore the sense of pace, and how different paces feel in the body.

Another form which is all about responding in the moment is dance improvisation. Find a class in which the teacher will guide you through exercises to help to explore and broaden your range of movement (independentdance.co.uk). There's also 'contact improvisation', where you explore movement in contact with another dancer – rolling, falling, supporting and giving weight to a partner. Those who practise it describe it as an 'art-sport' in which muscle tension is released and you can let go into the natural flow of movement. Capoeira, the Brazilian martial-art-cum-dance, is also very much about exploring movement in each moment, within the framework of a highly athletic set of forms. There is now a lively London Capoeira scene with schools throughout the city.

Try this: mindful at the gym

The gym is a place where everything seems geared to cranking up the pace. Pumping music and TV screens are here to distract you from the hard work and the muscle pain. But if you actively focus on what you are doing, you are more likely to get the most from each exercise and not injure yourself.

- As you train, try bringing awareness to the sensations in the muscles being worked, and to your breath. If it's a shoulder press, feel your out breath as you push the weight overhead. How do your shoulder muscles feel at the top, and when you return them to the start position? Is there a difference in the sensations of relaxed and contracted muscles?

- Feel the contact of your hands or feet with the equipment as you move through your training sets. Notice tensions in your body, and notice when your heart rate increases.

- Check in with yourself: how does your body feel as a whole? Are you tired or energised? Is your body happy to be challenged further, or is it telling you to stop? Sometimes injury occurs when repetitions are too fast, so with mindfulness you can find the right pace, paying attention to your body instead of overriding it with your mind.

FINDING THE RIGHT PACE

Can you be mindful at any speed? I think the short answer is yes, as many top athletes would testify. We can be sure that Usain Bolt is completely focused and present for those 9.6 seconds it takes him to run the 100 metres. Tennis players have to be 'in the zone' as they leap around the court, and when their anxieties and emotions distract them we see it on their faces – and in the score. Meditation is part of the training for many athletes, and a number of stars of fast-paced sports like football, baseball and basketball say they meditate regularly to help focus their minds.

We can be mindful when we're cycling or skating, and we can enjoy the feeling of speed in its right place. One of my own passions is flying down a hill on a pair of skis, which demands being fully present with the movement and the mountain – if I drift off I might find myself on my backside. Carl Honoré, a fellow Londoner and author of *In Praise of Slow*, says he loves to play two of the fastest sports: ice hockey and squash. Carl says that speed has its place in the modern world, but the problem occurs when speed becomes a way of life, and we get 'stuck in fast forward'. He uses a musical metaphor to suggest that what we need is to find the right pace in each moment – the *tempo giusto*.

So we can be mindful at any pace, but if most Londoners are honest, if we're missing one thing in our life, it is not more speed. Speed in itself may be fine, but we may feel a constant sense of hurry and rush: speed with an extra ingredient of anxiety. With the stress of commuting and working and cramming everything in, we may find that our nervous system cranks up and never rests. We get stuck in the 'fight or flight' mode of hyper-arousal: adrenaline pumping, heart rate elevated, muscles tensed, feeling on constant alert. Life is one big race, and we're running from morning to night with one eye on the clock.

If this sounds familiar, it could be time to make room for more changes of pace – to balance moments of speed with moments of slowness and even stillness. This can be challenging: when the body is pumping with adrenaline, it often feels uncomfortable to slow down, and that buzzy, agitated feeling can take time to settle. For this reason, many people who practise meditation like to start with stretching, walking or a gentle jog as a way of 'winding down' before sitting still. Some of the Eastern movement practices like yoga grew up historically as a way of calming down and directing the energies of the body in preparation for the stillness of meditation. Each of us has a different body, so we can experiment with what it needs. The *tempo giusto* may be different from day to day and from moment to moment, and the key to finding it is to bring mindfulness into our body as we move through our day.

MINDFUL GUIDE

Yoga and Pilates

THE LIFE CENTRE

The Life Centre has studios in Notting Hill and Islington. It is one of London's oldest dedicated yoga centres, with a high quality of teaching. The original Notting Hill centre is situated in a converted chapel on a quiet road, with a main studio and a smaller loft. The Islington centre opened in 2011, with two large, bright studios in a converted warehouse. Both offer a full schedule of classes from morning to night, seven days a week, as well as workshops by leading visiting teachers run in partnership with Yogacampus, their education arm. Visit their website for a good explanation of the various yoga styles, from powerful Ashtanga to slower forms like Gentle Yoga and Restorative Yoga.

thelifecentre.com
15 Edge Street, W8 7PN
1 Britannia Row, N1 8HQ

TRIYOGA

Triyoga is a big player on the London yoga and Pilates scene, with four studios offering a wide range of styles and many high-profile teachers. The original centre opened in 2000 in Primrose Hill, followed by studios in Covent Garden, Soho and Chelsea. There are therapy rooms where you can indulge in complementary treatments such as acupuncture, reflexology, reiki and Indian head massage. The in-house shops sell mats, clothing and yoga books, and the cafés at Primrose Hill and Chelsea offer fresh juices and various wholesome foods for a pre- or post-yoga snack.

triyoga.co.uk
6 Erskine Road, NW3 3AJ

—

YOGA PLACE

Yoga Place is a hub for yoga in East London with a friendly, unpretentious atmosphere. Stepping in off busy Bethnal Green Road and heading up the staircase, you'll find a surprisingly peaceful haven. There's an emphasis on the dynamic Ashtanga style of yoga, but they offer classes across the board including Gentle Yoga, relaxed Hatha Yoga classes and meditation. Classes are drop-in, so there's no need to book ahead (except for special courses), just turn up in good time.

yogaplace.co.uk
1st Floor, 449–453 Bethnal Green Road, E2 9QH

—

INDABA

Indaba opened its doors in Marylebone in 2011, with the aim of offering high-quality teaching in a plethora of styles. As with the other studios listed here, they teach everything from more meditative classes like Yin Yoga (holding postures for a long time) to dynamic forms like Ashtanga, Dharma Mittra and Power Asana. Ranging over four storeys, Indaba has three yoga studios with high ceilings and beautiful parquet

floors, as well as therapy rooms for massage and bodywork.

indabayoga.com
18 Hayes Place, NW1 6UA

—

EVOLVE WELLNESS CENTRE

Evolve has a timetable of yoga classes of all flavours, but its founders are also keen to develop a wider remit including workshops and talks on self-development, leadership, wellbeing and the environment. The Centre is located in a cobbled mews in South Kensington, with bright studios, treatment rooms and a seminar room. Special events include gong baths, city retreats and 'wilderness spas', involving group trips to Epping Forrest for meditative activities in nature.

evolvewellnesscentre.com
10 Kendrick Mews, SW7 3HG

—

PILATES FOUNDATION

Pilates uses whole body movement to target imbalances, strengthening muscles and retraining movement patterns. Practised well, it can bring a heightened sense of awareness and ease to the body. The Pilates Foundation website has a class finder where you can search by postcode for a teacher near you.

pilatesfoundation.com

—

Slow motion: Tai Chi and Qigong

TAI CHI NEAR YOU

Tai Chi is an ancient Chinese method of self-development which uses a flowing sequence of movements called the Form. It is said to improve health, increase energy, relieve stress and focus the mind. To try it out, Tai Chi Finder is a useful website where you can plug in your street name and find classes nearby. Or check the Tai Chi News website, run by London's largest Tai Chi school, the Mei Quan Academy. They teach the most widely practised 'Yang style', with classes in 36 locations across the city. Their classes incorporate Qigong, including the beautifully named '8 Pieces of Silk Brocade' sequence, breathing exercises and standing meditation postures.

Most Tai Chi classes take place in schools, church halls and community centres, but a few organisations have their own centres. Master Ding Academy has a purpose-built training centre overlooking Limehouse Basin Marina in Docklands, with classes throughout the week.

taichifinder.co.uk
taichinews.com
masterdingacademy.com

—

QIGONG NEAR YOU

The College of Elemental Chi Kung has information on teachers running Qigong classes around London, and workshops based on the five elements, linked to the energies of the body. The Simon

Lau Centre in South Kensington teaches Qigong along with Martial Arts. The Lam Association – run by Master Lam Kamchuen, author of the groundbreaking work *The Way of Energy* – offers regular classes from its base in Lambeth North. Tai Chi organisations often include elements of Qigong in their classes, and the Tai Chi Finder website includes listings for Qigong.

taichifinder.co.uk
elementalchikung.com
simonlaucentre.co.uk
lamassociation.org

—

Swimming

HAMPSTEAD PONDS

These three wooded ponds on Hampstead Heath have been used for freshwater swimming since the mid-19th century. The Highgate Men's Pond is situated in a secluded spot and bathing costumes are optional. The Kenwood Ladies' Pond is highest up the hill, with the cleanest water, and hidden by foliage to protect the ladies' modesty. The Hampstead Mixed Pond gets busy in summer, but is still a lovely spot to cool off on a hot day.

The Ladies' and Men's Ponds are the UK's only life-guarded open-water swimming facilities open to the public every day of the year. The Corporation of London website posts regular information on water temperature and water quality tests. The ponds are for competent swimmers over 8, and 8- to 15-year-olds are permitted only with an accompanying adult. Swimmers wishing to use the Mixed Pond during the winter must join the Winter Swimming Club as there are no lifeguards then.

cityoflondon.gov.uk/hampstead
Hampstead Heath, NW5 1QR

—

SERPENTINE LIDO

A fresh-water swim in the centre of London, complete with ducks and swans, weeds, and traditional sun loungers for hire. If you're brave enough to swim in winter, you can join the Serpentine Swimming Club, the oldest swimming club in Britain, which lets you swim in the lake from 6am to 9:30am year round.

royalparks.org.uk/parks/hyde-park/
sport-in-hyde-park/serpentine-lido
serpentineswimmingclub.com
Serpentine South Side, Hyde Park
W2 2UH

—

TOOTING BEC LIDO
Tooting Bec Lido is Britain's largest outdoor freshwater pool, at just over 90 metres long. It opened in 1906 and is still a delightfully retro experience, with its brightly coloured changing huts and vast expanse of Technicolor blue. On hot summer weekends and holidays it is packed with kids, but try a weekday up to 8pm for a quieter swim after work. In winter the pool is open every day to members of the South London Swimming Club, which anyone can join. Surrounded by trees,

it's like swimming in a lake, with temperatures to match – never warm, but definitely invigorating.

dcleisurecentres.co.uk/centres/
tooting-bec-lido/
slsc.org.uk
Tooting Bec Road, SW16 1RU

—

OUTDOOR SWIMMING SOCIETY
The OSS is for people who like to swim outside in lakes, ponds and rivers rather than in chlorinated pools. Their social events usually include a winter plunge in a London Lido. Most usefully, their wild swim map shows outdoor swimming locations in London and nearby counties.

outdoorswimmingsociety.com
wildswim.com

—

LONDON AQUATICS CENTRE

In 2014 the stunning London Aquatics Centre, the swimming and diving venue for the 2012 Olympics, opened its doors for public swimming. There's a huge 50-metre, 10-lane 'competition' pool designated for lane-swimming, and another 50-metre 'training' pool which is mainly for schools and families. With prices the same or less than a local pool, and long opening hours, it should soon become a regular destination for East End swimmers, and a periodic treat for the rest of us. Since the Games, the spectator wings have been removed and 2,800 square metres of glass has been installed to allow much more natural light into the building. It's like swimming inside a sculpture made of light and undulating glass. Architect Zaha Hadid's beautiful wave-like structure creates one of the world's most inspiring places to enjoy the experience of swimming.

better.org.uk/leisure/london-aquatics-centre

Queen Elizabeth Olympic Park, E20 2ZQ

—

Running

RUNNING MEDITATION

Mindful running is not yet a big movement in London, but there's a book on the subject by the head of Shambhala, an international meditation network which has a centre in Clapham. Sakyong Mipham is a meditation master, nine-time marathon runner and author of the book, *Running with the Mind of Meditation*. He describes meditative running as a way to synchronise your body and mind so you can become healthier and more joyful in every moment. When you are more fully in your body, your movement becomes more fluid, you are less likely to injure yourself and you can appreciate your environment. Not only do you become a better runner, but your life begins to exude balance and strength. The London Shambhala Meditation

Centre holds occasional workshops based on this approach.

shambhala.org.uk/running.php

—

BAREFOOT RUNNING

Barefoot runners say that running is more natural and mindful if you cast off your thick padded trainers in favour of thin flexible shoes, or completely bare feet. After running in shoes, the skills of barefoot running take time to learn, and practice. Several London coaches offer workshops and private training in this approach.

runtobecome.com
barefootperformanceacademy.com
barefootrunninguk.com

—

Dance

5RHYTHMS

5Rhythms offers classes and open workshops where you can explore your own expression within a format developed by dance teacher Gabrielle Roth. Each session progresses through five kinds of rhythm which encourage different ways of moving: a kind of moving meditation where you're encouraged to be fully present in the body in each moment. There are over 300 certified 5Rhythms teachers worldwide, and a number running regular sessions in London. Visit the international 5Rhythms website to find local teachers, or try one of the other London-based sites below.

5rhythms.com
dancingtao.net
acalltodance.com
emmadance.co.uk

—

INDEPENDENT DANCE

Independent Dance offers classes and workshops with a focus on exploring movement. Their regular Monday night improvisation class is open to all levels, and led by different teachers each week. Weekday morning classes are for experienced movement practitioners, with teachers bringing in approaches from a range of disciplines such as Feldenkrais, Chi Gong, Akido and so on. Classes take place at the Siobhan Davies Studios.

independentdance.co.uk
Siobhan Davies Studios, 85 St George's Road, SEI 6ER

—

LONDON CONTACT IMPROVISATION

Contact Improvisation is a dance form developed in the 1970s, based on two or more bodies exploring movement in communication, using physical contact. London Contact Improvisation offers regular classes and 'jams' for all levels of experience. Most of their classes are based at Moving East, a centre for dance, martial arts and complementary medicine in Stoke Newington.

contactimprovisation.co.uk
movingeast.co.uk

St Matthias Church Hall, Wordsworth Road, NI6 8DD

—

CAPOEIRA

Capoeira is a game between two people, so once you've learnt the physical vocabulary it's about responding in each moment. First developed by the African slaves of Brazil, it combines elements of dance, martial arts and acrobatics. In recent years it has taken off in London, with numerous schools offering classes across the city.

londonschoolofcapoeira.com
capoeira.co.uk
capoeiracademyuk.com

—

LEARNING
AND
PRACTISING
MINDFULNESS

Mindfulness is a state of mind, or a way of being. It is also a set of practices which nurture that way of being. If we're interested in developing a more mindful life, it helps to keep both of these aspects in balance. Much of this book has been about developing the more informal aspects of mindfulness – finding ways to be more present within the maelstrom of London life. But to increase our ability to be present, it also helps us to have a formal practice. This is what develops our mindfulness muscles, strengthening our ability to notice when we are not really here and our ability to keep coming back.

I often meet people who feel very connected to the idea of mindfulness, who read books, watch videos and talk about the ideas, but find it hard to make space for the actual practices. It can be a bit like reading fitness articles but not doing any exercise: the reading won't help much when we need to run for the bus. I know myself what this mode feels like. As a teacher I take it for granted that I am steeped in mindfulness practice, but sometimes for one reason or another I lose my routine for a few days and forget or neglect my practice. When this happens I can start to feel the difference very quickly – I feel more foggy, less centred, less resilient to irritation and anxiety. As soon as I sit down to practise again, even for ten minutes, there's a feeling of healthiness and relief – 'ahhh, that's better'. It doesn't mean that difficulties immediately disappear, but there's a sense of nurturing the presence and strength which helps me to weather them.

You can get started with mindfulness on your own, following the instructions in books like this, or using audio and video. However, at some point if you're interested in taking it forward, it's good to have the support of a teacher, and to meet with other people who are practising. Mindfulness is deceptively simple, but when we start to get familiar with the workings of our thoughts, emotions and sensations there's an extraordinary range of experiences which can come up. Some may be pleasant, many will be challenging. You may feel like you are the only person who is unable to sit still and follow your breath, the worst meditator in the world, the only one who suffers from boredom, frustration or difficult emotions. By discussing your practice with others you'll discover much common ground, and learn how to work with challenges as they arise.

As we develop mindfulness, we start to become more familiar with the patterns of our own mind. We might see how we get caught up again and again in certain kinds of thought, having conversations with ourselves that we believe are real. 'He always does that; She doesn't like me; I am hopeless at this; I wish I had this...' Often we let these narratives fill up our reality and drive the way we behave. When we practise mindfulness, we can start to make friends with the thoughts and see their patterns. We're not trying to get rid of them to achieve an empty mind. Thoughts are natural, like waves, rising and falling within the sea of our awareness. But through meditation practice, start to discover the possibility that they are not so solid, and they are not our 'self'. We practise noticing them and gently letting them go, and through this practice they begin to loosen their hold on us.

Try this: mindfulness of thoughts

* **Mindfulness of breath**: Begin by sitting in a comfortable upright posture, feeling the contact of your feet on the ground and your bottom on the seat. Practise a few minutes of mindful breathing, paying attention to the physical sensations of the breath wherever you feel them. You don't have to change the breathing in any way, just be with it as it is. When your mind wanders, bring it gently back to the breath. (For more detailed instructions on mindful breathing, see Chapter 1.)

* **Mindfulness of sounds**: Now gently let go of your focus on the breath and shift the main focus of your awareness to sounds. You could imagine you are a microphone, letting the sounds come to you without bias. When you get caught up in *thoughts about* the sounds, see if you can come back to the direct experience of hearing: the tone, texture, volume, and so on. Notice the way sounds come and go within a bigger space – the vast space of your awareness. (See Chapter 6 for more detail on mindfulness of sounds.)

* **Mindfulness of thoughts**: Now let go of the sounds and shift the focus of your awareness to thoughts. Instead of thinking being a distraction, now you can let thoughts come centre stage. You

could imagine that your mind is the blue sky – clear and spacious – and the thoughts are like clouds coming and going. Some may be heavy and thick, some small and wispy. Notice when you get completely caught up in a thought, and come back to the sense of the bigger sky. Notice how thoughts are coming and going in the vast space of your awareness, just like the sounds did. Some may come with an emotional charge, like an electrical storm in the body. Some may flit by. See if you can be aware of these different qualities and the changing weather.

• **Mindfulness of breath**: Return your awareness to the breath, feeling it in the body. Let the breath breathe itself, and rest your mind in its natural rhythm.

This can be quite a challenging practice, so don't worry if you find it difficult. The main point is to nurture your interest and curiosity about thoughts. When we are caught up in them, they seem very real, and they can fill the whole world. But are they as solid as we think? Don't look for quick or certain answers, but see if you can nurture a friendly, inquisitive approach to the workings of your own mind.

MINDFULNESS COURSES: MBSR AND MBCT

The most widely recognised courses for mindfulness are known as MBSR (Mindfulness-Based Stress Reduction) and MBCT (Mindfulness-Based Cognitive Therapy). They are closely related, and as a participant you would notice little difference between the two courses, normally presented over eight weeks. Both have been the subject of numerous research studies by the international medical community, showing a wide range of benefits for health and wellbeing. If you have a mental health issue such as depression or an anxiety disorder, you could choose to look for an MBCT course run by a clinical psychologist, which may sometimes offer more specific help working with your particular challenges. Please note that although mindfulness can be very helpful for people dealing with recurrent patterns of depression, it is not recommended if you're right in the midst of a severe and overwhelming depression – do talk with the teacher about your situation before you join. For the majority of mindfulness participants, there's no need to worry too much about the choice between acronyms, the main thing is to find a convenient location and a qualified teacher. There is currently no regulatory body for mindfulness teachers, but the course should be run by a person who has done mindfulness training with a reputable body such as Bangor or Oxford Universities, and who follows the Good-practice Guidelines (mindfulnessteachersuk.org.uk).

London has seen an explosion of mindfulness courses in the past few years, and it's likely you can find a course which is near your home or workplace. The Mental Health Foundation's Be Mindful website allows you to search for courses by postcode (bemindful. co.uk). London employers are also increasingly investing in mindfulness workshops and courses for their staff. You could think about persuading your own workplace to host a session as part of their wellbeing or staff development programme.

MEDITATION CENTRES

Mindfulness in London takes place as a network of teachers and courses across the city, mainly using hired venues rather than occupying a permanent base. There are also spaces which are dedicated places for meditation, where you can drop in more informally. These meditation centres are mainly Buddhist in origin, although they are welcoming to all comers, and many who practise there wouldn't call themselves Buddhist or adhere to any particular belief system.

Buddhism is the spiritual tradition which is generally closest to the secular practice of mindfulness. Jon Kabat-Zinn, American founder of MBSR, was a practitioner of Zen, and it was on retreat with the Vietnamese Zen teacher Thich Nhat Hanh that he came up with the inspiration that mindfulness could help people with chronic medical conditions. This was the seed which grew into the current mindfulness movement. Mindfulness meditation gets from Buddhism its orientation towards being present with our experience as it is, rather than going off into any kind of altered state, which can be the aim of some other meditation systems.

London has a wealth of spiritual traditions, with a range of goals and practices, but in this chapter I'll feature centres which practise something close to secular mindfulness. At most of London's Buddhist centres, meditation is understood as a natural and important human skill, which can be learned without becoming a Buddhist or having an interest in Buddhist teachings. In fact, Buddha simply means 'the awakened one', and the historical Buddha was called this because he discovered how to live a life that was fully awake. The figure of the Buddha can be a symbol of how to become more awake, present and mindful in our own lives. If this idea has resonance for you, it's a symbol you could choose to appreciate without worrying that you are signing up to any particular creed.

There are also traditions of Christian meditation which share much in common with mindfulness meditation. For instance, the Benedictine monk John Main developed a method of silent meditation through studying the teachings of the earliest Christian monks. Such forms of silent meditation or prayer were practised by Christian mystics like the anonymous author of the 14th-century English spiritual classic *The Cloud of Unknowing,* and are now practised in small groups across London. In the 17th century, the Quakers (or Society of Friends) developed their own form of silent worship, which is followed in Friends' meetings around the city. Other spiritual traditions, including Islam, Hinduism and Judaism, have meditative practices, sometimes silent and sometimes using chanting, prayer, movement and other forms of expression. Some of these traditions have slightly different aims from mindfulness meditation, such as reaching a particular spiritual state or communicating with God, which are beyond the scope of this book. However, if you have a connection with one of these traditions, do find your own way to explore its relationship to the experience of mindfulness we've been talking about.

MAKING FRIENDS WITH THE CITY

Most of us come to mindfulness looking for a respite, a little oasis of peace within our busy lives. However, once it starts to seep into our system, we might find that it's not just about getting away from other people into a soft white cocoon with soothing music and incense. In fact, we might notice the opposite – that actually we become more interested and engaged with other people and the world around us. Our usual mental chatter keeps us fixated on ourselves and our important problems, which occupy the centre of the universe. When we stop being quite so wrapped up in this chatter, we open up to a bigger world, and we can feel more friendly and open to others. Perhaps we start to notice the person serving us at the checkout, or the colleague at work who is having a hard time, or the pregnant woman waiting for a seat on the Tube.

It's easy to become a misanthrope when you live in a crowded city. On the Underground, or a rush-hour bus, other human beings are obstacles; sources of discomfort and claustrophobia. However, if you can make a small mental shift, these can also be places to appreciate the incredible diversity of Londoners and urban life. This sense of greater warmth towards others is something that often happens naturally with mindfulness, but we also nurture it more intentionally.

Try this: people-watching

Next time you're on the Tube, bus or train, instead of frittering away your mental energy on reading the ads or playing games on your phone, see what it's like to deliberately cultivate your interest in other human beings. Here are a few ideas:

* Imagine you are a portrait artist. Look at the faces around you. Whose portrait would you paint? What traits would you try to capture?

- If you were a writer, which characters would you put in your novel? Or who would you invite to dinner? Instead of letting this take you into a daydream, use these questions (or your own version) to help you be interested, look around, and be present.

- Are there people you find boring or repellent? Instead of blanking them, could you be a little more curious about them? Perhaps that man looks sour because his wife recently left him and he's unhappy. Maybe that elderly woman is in constant pain. If someone irritates you, see if it's possible to make a small shift towards understanding.

- Look around at the people playing with their phones, listening on headphones or staring into space. Are any of your fellow travellers actually present in the carriage or bus as you are now? Ask this not in order to have a sense of superiority, but to notice the difference between being present and being absent, which is also part of your own experience.

This is an exercise you could also do in any place where there are people – sitting in a café, waiting in a bank, or on a bench in a busy park. When you notice you are drifting into constant low-level irritation at the rest of the world, see if it's possible to nurture a more friendly and interested approach.

MINDFUL GUIDE

Mindfulness courses

BE MINDFUL

The Mental Health Foundation hosts a website where you can search by location for courses across the UK, including many in London. There's also a directory of resources and an online stress test.

bemindful.co.uk

—

BEING MINDFUL

I am co-director of this small south London organisation offering mindfulness courses and coaching. We also lead sessions in workplaces including organisations like Transport for London, the University of Westminster, the Mental Health Foundation and various charities, local councils, health organisations, schools, colleges and libraries.

beingmindful.co.uk

BREATHING SPACE

Breathing Space is run by the London Buddhist Centre, based in Bethnal Green. They teach mindfulness courses to help with mental health, including specialist courses for addiction recovery, retreats for carers in Tower Hamlets, and training programmes for mental health professionals. The director is NHS consultant psychiatrist, Dr Paramabandhu Groves.

breathingspacelondon.org.uk

—

MINDFULNESS LONDON

Ed Halliwell teaches mindfulness workshops and courses at The School of Life, near Russell Square, and also leads training in organisations. Ed is the co-author of *The Mindful Manifesto: How doing less and noticing more can help us thrive in a stressed-out world* (2010).

mindfulnesslondon.co.uk
workwithmindfulness.com

MIND FREE

Christopher Gaia runs mindfulness courses in Chelsea, as well as introductory seminars and one-to-one sessions.

mindfree.co.uk

—

OPTIMAL LIVING

Mindfulness courses led by Peter and Rosalie in central London and Blackheath. One-to-one courses and distance learning are available.

optimalliving.co.uk

—

MBSR.CO.UK

Mindfulness courses in London and Birmingham are led or supervised by Michael Chaskalson, one of the UK's leading mindfulness teachers and author of several books, including *The Mindful Workplace*. The London courses take place in central locations.

mbsr.co.uk

LONDON CENTRE FOR MINDFULNESS

These MBSR courses are based at the Jamyang Buddhist Centre in Kennington, but are run in a non-religious framework.

londoncentreformindfulness.com

—

LONDON MEDITATION

Group courses in MBSR and MBCT, as well as individual mindfulness coaching, are led by Susann Herrmann and Albert Tobler in Camden, north London.

london-meditation.co.uk

—

LEARN MINDFULNESS

Shamash Aldina, author of *Mindfulness for Dummies*, teaches courses in several London locations, including Stoke Newington and Chelsea.

learnmindfulness.co.uk

THE MINDFULNESS PROJECT

London's first dedicated space for secular mindfulness offers courses and drop-in sessions in Fitzroy Square near Warren Street.

londonmindful.com

—

Meditation centres and groups

LONDON SHAMBHALA MEDITATION CENTRE

Drop in any Monday or Wednesday evening for free meditation instruction at this Clapham-based centre, part of the global Shambhala network founded by Chögyam Trungpa Rinpoche. The beautiful meditation hall has high ceilings and white walls with vivid Tibetan banners, creating a spacious and wakeful setting for practice. While it has roots in Buddhism, Shambhala has a strong tradition of teaching meditation as a natural human skill. It is seen as a way to discover one's innate

clarity and confidence, and to create a more wakeful society. As well as drop-in sessions, there is a programme of structured courses, weekend retreats and contemplative arts such as photography, flower arranging, voice work and visual art.

shambhala.org.uk
27 Belmont Close, SW4 6AY

—

WAKE UP LONDON AND HEART OF LONDON SANGHA

Wake Up London brings together young people, aged 16 to 35, for Saturday afternoon sessions to meditate and nurture mindfulness in everyday life. This lively group has organised flash mobs – open to all – in busy London locations like Trafalgar Square and Covent Garden. The people who take part in them are not just there for the practice itself, but to join in a public statement about the power and importance of meditation. Wake Up London is linked to the Heart of London Sangha, a community for all ages which practises mindfulness in the tradition of the Vietnamese Zen master Thich Nhat Hanh. Their Saturday morning sessions consist of silent, guided and walking meditation, listening to a talk, and discussion. They also have smaller groups in Dulwich, north London and Richmond.

wakeuplondon.org
hols.org.uk
Friends Meeting House, 8 Hop

—

TRIRATNA BUDDHIST CENTRES

The Triratna Buddhist community is an international movement (previously known as the FWBO) founded by British teacher Sangharakshita. Its flagship centre in Bethnal Green is housed in a converted red-brick Victorian fire station, with several meditation rooms, large golden Buddha statues and a bookshop. There are lunchtime drop-in sessions, evening classes, courses on

Buddhist themes and special groups for men, women and young people; mainly at low cost or for a small suggested donation. Their other London centres include the North London centre in Holloway, the West London centre near Westbourne Park, the Croydon Centre and several smaller groups.

lbc.org.uk
northlondonbuddhistcentre.com
westlondonbuddhistcentre.com
buddhistcentrecroydon.org
51 Roman Road, E2 0HU

—

KAGYU SAMYE DZONG

The former Bermondsey Library in Spa Road opened as a meditation centre in 2010. The beautiful spaces of the former library have been transformed into colourful shrine rooms. Resident ordained monks and nuns add to the atmosphere of a traditional Tibetan monastery. The Centre is rooted in the Kagyu Tibetan Buddhist lineage and offers a programme of courses focusing on meditation, Buddhism, holistic therapies and Tibetan martial arts. There's a welcoming Tibetan Tea Room, a shop and a treatment room. Kagyu Samye Dzong has a second centre at Manor Place in Elephant and Castle, in a former public baths and wash-house, which hosts a smaller programme of courses in its more intimate shrine room.

london.samye.org
15 Spa Road, SE16 3SA
33 Manor Place, SE17 3BD

—

JAMYANG BUDDHIST CENTRE

Jamyang is located in the beautiful Old Courthouse in Kennington, built in 1869. The wood-panelled rooms with colourful thangkas and statues create a warm, rich environment for practice. Some introductory meditation classes are offered, along with a wider programme of Buddhist teachings. The courtyard hosts the lovely Courtyard Garden Café, which serves home-cooked lunches, coffee and cake. Jamyang

is affiliated to the Foundation for the Preservation of the Mahayana Tradition (FPMT), an international organisation based on the Gelugpa tradition, the school of Tibetan Buddhism associated with the Dalai Lama.

jamyang.co.uk
The Old Courthouse, 43 Renfrew Road, SE11 4NA

—

LONDON INSIGHT MEDITATION

London Insight Meditation promotes approaches to meditation drawn from early Buddhism, but they emphasise that you do not have to be a Buddhist to practise them. Linked to Gaia House retreat centre in Devon, the group does not have a physical centre, but runs workshops and courses in a number of venues. See the website for dates, locations and times. Meditation days take place frequently at King Alfred School in Golders Green, north London. There are also local sitting groups

which meet in people's homes
around the city.

londoninsight.org

—

CHRISTIAN MEDITATION

The World Community for
Christian Meditation practises
contemplative prayer in the form
of silent meditation, as passed on
through the teaching of Benedictine
monk John Main (1926–1982). Their
approach involves the repetition
of a single word, an ancient way
of bringing the mind to rest in the
heart. In their weekly groups they
welcome all who come, and in the
silence it is also fine to follow your
own individual practice. They see
a close connection between their
form of prayer and mindfulness
meditation, with an emphasis on
acceptance, rather than seeking
an altered state of consciousness.
There are dozens of Christian
Meditation groups in London.

christianmeditation.org.uk

LONDON QUAKERS

The Quakers, also known as the
Society of Friends, practise a
350-year-old form of worship
which is mainly silent. There
are no set prayers or clergy, but
individuals may speak when they
feel moved to do so. Here silence
is valued as a place in which to wait
for guidance from an inner voice,
which for them is the experience
of God. There are about 40 groups
across London, most of them
meeting weekly on Sundays, and
some more or less often.

londonquakers.org.uk

—

A FEW FINAL THOUGHTS

A MINDFUL LONDON?

As mindfulness gains in popularity, many who discover its benefits as individuals are starting to explore how it might be transformative for society as a whole. With stress and depression on the rise, we can no longer take our society's mental health for granted. We're working longer, crazier hours: six in ten of British employees regularly work beyond their contracted hours, putting in an average of 1.5 hours' overtime a day, and nearly one in four of us claim to work an extra two or three hours a day. Not surprisingly, stress is the most common cause of long-term sickness leave. Meanwhile, UK doctors are writing five times as many prescriptions for anti-depressants as they were ten years ago. The World Health Organisation predicts that by 2030 depression will be the biggest health problem on the planet.

In this human pressure cooker, many believe that mindfulness is the thing we are most missing – the cool balm to pour on our agitation and speed. Since 2004, the National Institute for Health and Care Excellence recommends mindfulness as a better way than drugs to treat repeat-episode depression, although it is taking time for courses to become widely known and available. Welsh MP Chris Ruane is a tireless spokesman for mindfulness in Parliament, and has even got MPs doing mindfulness courses within the hallowed halls of Westminster. The Mindfulness in Schools project is bringing mindfulness into the curriculum, helping teenagers to cope with stress, concentrate better and feel more content.

Meanwhile, organisations are discovering mindfulness as a core skill their staff need to help them thrive in a world of challenge and change. Mindfulness is increasingly taught to managers and staff in leading London workplaces, including Transport for London, Barclays, Lloyds, Prudential, GlaxoSmithKline, eBay, the Cabinet Office and the Home Office. This training has been shown again and again to bring measurable benefits, including resilience to stress and depression, improved performance, better relationships with colleagues and greater job satisfaction.

As well as formal mindfulness training, there are also many ways to support a more mindful environment, such as 'no-email days', designing spaces for relaxation and quiet, and creating an atmosphere where staff feel it's okay to take proper breaks away from their desks. Our mindless habits have a strong momentum: we can slip so easily into hours of unproductive stupor on the computer, or crank ourselves up into a frenzy of hurry where tempers are lost and mistakes are made. By learning to pause and pay more attention in each moment we can actually be more productive, as well as enjoy what we are doing. Individually and collectively we can start to discover what kinds of environments help us to feel more spacious and less frazzled. Together we can explore how to create more mindful workplaces, homes and neighbourhoods, and a more mindful city.

JOURNEY WITHOUT A MAP

London is one of the world's most creative communities, and it is exciting to see how many Londoners are engaged in this challenge in many different ways – not always involving 'mindfulness' as such, but often in a mindful spirit. Everywhere we see experiments to create sane, friendly, relaxing, imaginative environments, from cafés to yoga studios to galleries to gardens – many of which are reflected in this book. Hopefully you have found in *Mindful London* some ideas about places and practices to help you to slow down, reflect and replenish within the maelstrom of London life.

The emphasis in this book has been on ways to calm and quiet the mind, and this is deeply needed. But as you explore mindfulness, you may discover that it is even more powerful than that. Over time our minds get into deeply ingrained habits, and mindfulness works by gently loosening our grip on these, opening us up to a vast world of possibility. Slowly we might find ourselves letting go of some of our fixed ideas about who we are and what we like, and as a result feeling more inquisitive, joyful and alive.

You could think of it as like a journey through London. You get used to your familiar route: Northern line, change at Stockwell, Victoria line to Oxford Circus, change to the Central line – you can do it in your sleep. You start to forget that the Tube map is a schematic diagram, and the city doesn't really look this way. With mindfulness, suddenly you find yourself thrown out above ground without a map. You might be in a part of the city you've never visited. In the distance you may see some familiar landmarks – The Shard rising up, or Centre Point, or Canary Wharf. But here you are with no A–Z, no smartphone, and today there is no rush to get anywhere. Should you hop on this bus, or walk down this alleyway, or step into this intriguing café? You feel free to wander and discover new neighbourhoods.

Italo Calvino's classic *Invisible Cities* presents vignettes of imaginary cities, each embodying different states of mind, or ways of being human. For us living in London, the city is a constant reflection of our own mental world. One day we may be living in a noisy, chaotic, aggressive, infuriating, degraded metropolis, the next we are in a magnificent, exhilarating, inspiring, eclectic, beautiful world capital. It's the same city, only our minds have changed. With mindfulness, we can slowly shift the balance from discontent to appreciation and enjoyment.

A MINDFUL REVOLUTION: IN THIS MOMENT

Mindfulness is a training, or retraining, in the art of living life as it's happening. It's a simple, ancient human skill, but it is needed now more than ever before. As each new technology seduces us further into virtual worlds, and as the pace increasingly accelerates, mindfulness puts on the brakes and invites us to stop and be present.

Here are five things you can do to be mindful in this moment. You can do these as a sequence, or any one of them can be enough to bring you into the present. Take a few minutes to read through the list and try the suggestions.

- **Slow down**: Notice your speed. Have you been rushing? Do you need to? Feel what the sense of hurry is like in your body – are there jittery feelings somewhere, agitation, adrenaline? How does your body feel when you let it settle?

- **Notice without judgement**: How are you feeling right now? Are you spending your energy resisting something about your situation, wanting things to be different? See if you can let go of struggle and relax with how things actually are.

- **Feel the ground**: Bring your full attention to the contact of your feet on the floor. If you're sitting, feel your bottom on the seat. Let the weight of your body be supported by the earth.

- **Breathe**: Take a few conscious breaths, feeling the physical sensations somewhere in your body. Let your breath breathe itself, and rest your awareness on its natural rhythm.

- **Enjoy one sense fully**: Look up and around. Or listen to the sounds arising and dissolving. Or bring your attention to the taste of food or drink. Pick one of your senses and give it your full attention.

Is there one thing on this list which resonates most for you right now? Make that your mantra, reminding yourself to do it as often as you can, for the rest of today, or even the rest of this week. And as you go about your life, let London itself be a reminder to wake up and be present: the sounds, the buildings, the trees, the people, the richness and chaotic energy of the big city.

Mindfulness is the missing key to living a more content, more fulfilled life in the 21st century. This key is something we hold in our hands in each moment. Each moment we have a choice to open the door from claustrophobia and anxiety into spaciousness and enjoyment. May this book be a small inspiration to start, here and now, with your own mindful revolution.

Acknowledgements

I'd like to thank all the participants in my Being Mindful classes for sharing their experience of bringing mindfulness into their busy London lives. In particular, thanks to Steve Smith, Scott Kirk, Adrian Bethune, Jim Coakes, Sian Griffin and John Lawlor for their contributions. I'm grateful to Jane Ward, Lisa Oestreicher, Annalie Wilson and Sylvester Laciok for advice and ideas, and to all my friends and fellow meditators at the London Shambhala Meditation Centre.

Many thanks to my Being Mindful colleague Debbie Johnson for sharing this journey with me, and to my mentor Cindy Cooper for her wisdom and support. My yoga teachers Graham Burns and Susanne Lahusen have helped me discover more each week about mindful movement. Many ideas in this book have come from my experience of running Slow Down London, and I'm deeply grateful to my co-founders Deepa Patel and Amanda Stone; and to Carl Honoré and Mohit Bakaya for sharing their ideas for slowing down.

Thank you to Elen Jones for her vision in commissioning this book, to my agent Steph Ebdon, and to the staff at Virgin Books. My appreciation to Helena Caldon for her copy editing, Jilly Topping for the elegant design and Brett Ryder for his beautiful illustrations.

Thanks to my two wonderful daughters Katrina and Tanya, and to my inspiring father Frank Watt. Finally, special thanks to my husband Richard Woolley for his constant support, his keen editing eye, and his natural mindfulness in caring for the details of daily life.

FURTHER MINDFULNESS RESOURCES

BOOKS

Mindfulness: A Practical Guide to Finding Peace in a Frantic World by Mark Williams and Danny Penman (Piatkus, 2011). One of the founders of Mindfulness-based Cognitive Therapy, Professor Mark Williams of Oxford University leads you through an 8-week mindfulness programme, with a CD of guided practices.

Introducing Mindfulness: A Practical Guide by Tessa Watt (Icon 2012). A concise and accessible guide to mindfulness practice, packed with straightforward exercises and practical tips for bringing mindfulness into daily life.

The Mindful Manifesto: How Doing Less And Noticing More Can Help Us Thrive In A Stressed-Out World by Dr Jonty Heaversedge and Ed Halliwell (Hay House, 2010). How can mindfulness change society? An overview of research and practice, with an inspiring vision.

Sane New World: Taming the Mind by Ruby Wax (Hodder & Stoughton, 2013). Comedian Ruby Wax, who now has a Masters from Oxford in Mindfulness-based Cognitive Therapy, presents an honest, funny and moving manual to saner living.

Full Catastrophe Living: Using the Wisdom of Your Body and Mind to Face Stress, Pain and Illness by Jon Kabat-Zinn (Delta, 1990). Jon Kabat-Zinn, creator of the Mindfulness-based Stress Reduction programme, presents the benefits of mindfulness for health and wellbeing.

The Mindful Way through Depression by Mark Williams, John Teasdale, Zindel Segal and Jon Kabat-Zinn (Guilford Press, 2007). A guide for those struggling with depression, by the founders of Mindfulness-based Cognitive Therapy.

The Mindful Workplace: Developing Resilient Individuals and Resonant Organizations with MBSR by Michael Chaskalson

(Wiley-Blackwell, 2011). London's leading proponent of mindfulness in the workplace argues that we no longer have to choose between economic imperatives and human wellbeing.

Wherever You Go, There You Are. Mindfulness Meditation for Everyday Life by Jon Kabat-Zinn (Piatkus, 1994). Jon Kabat-Zinn's personal and poetic guide to a more mindful life.

Get Some Headspace by Andy Puddicombe (Hodder & Stoughton, 2011). The founder of a successful London-based project to demystify meditation argues that ten minutes a day of practice can have life-changing effects.

In Praise of Slow by Carl Honoré (Orion, 2005). This influential book by Carl Honoré, global spokesman for the slow movement, explores the notion of 'slow' in food, medicine, workplaces, city planning and other areas of life.

The Miracle of Mindfulness, by Thich Nhat Hanh (Rider, 1991). The great Vietnamese Buddhist teacher Thich Nhat Hanh encourages meditation practice through anecdotes and exercises.

Turning the Mind into an Ally by Sakyong Mipham (Riverhead, 2004). How to discover the natural peace and clarity of our minds through the practice of meditation. Sakyong Mipham is the leader of Shambhala, a global network of meditation centres.

Seeking the Heart of Wisdom: The Path of Insight Meditation by Jack Goldstein and Jack Kornfield (Shambhala, 1987). The teachings of Theravada Buddhism, rooted in Southeast Asia, are presented in an accessible context for Westerners.

Shambhala: The Sacred Path of the Warrior by Chögyam Trungpa (Shambhala, 2007). The Tibetan meditation master Chögyam Trungpa teaches how to live a life of fearlessness and goodness based on the Shambhala teachings, named for a legendary enlightened kingdom.

Taking the Leap: Freeing Ourselves from Old Habits and Fears by Pema Chödrön (Shambhala, 2010). Much-loved American meditation teacher Pema Chödrön teaches how to break free of destructive patterns in our life by learning to stay present and open.

Apps

BUDDHIFY
buddhify.com
This well-designed UK app helps busy urbanites bring mindfulness into daily life, with guided meditations to use when you are travelling, exercising, working online, waiting around and so on. There are helpful tips and tools to track your meditation time.

HEADSPACE
getsomeheadspace.com
Describing itself as 'the world's first gym membership for the mind', London-based Headspace was founded by former Buddhist monk Andy Puddicombe. The free programme offers ten days of ten-minute meditation practices and clever animations which explain how meditation works. After that you can pay for a wide range of more tailored content.

INSIGHT TIMER
insighttimer.com
A free app which helps you time your meditation session with the sound of Tibetan singing bowls. There are options to log your practice and to connect with others meditating worldwide.

THE MINDFULNESS APP
mindapps.se
This American app comes with guided meditation practices of varying lengths between 3 and 30 minutes, an option for silent meditation and a short body-scan practice.

Websites and organisations

BE MINDFUL ONLINE

bemindfulonline.com

This 4-week online course run by the Mental Health Foundation features video, audio and interactive exercises, presented by Tessa Watt and Ed Halliwell.

THE CENTRE FOR MINDFULNESS RESEARCH AND PRACTICE

bangor.ac.uk/mindfulness

Based at Bangor University, this is a leading provider of professional mindfulness training. It also offers public courses including a distance-learning programme and guided mindfulness meditation CDs.

GAIA HOUSE

gaiahouse.co.uk

Gaia House in South Devon offers retreats following various Buddhist traditions led by teachers from all over the world.

MINDFUL

mindful.org

News and features about mindfulness and 'mindful society'. There are features on projects in schools, offices, prisons and so on; practical tips; and updates on research.

MINDFULNESS-BASED COGNITIVE THERAPY (UK)

mbct.co.uk

The official UK website of MBCT contains resources and links.

MINDFULNESS MEDITATION PRACTICE CDS AND TAPES

mindfulnesstapes.com

A resource for CDs and downloads of guided mindfulness practices led by MBSR founder Jon Kabat-Zinn.

MINDFULNESS RESEARCH GUIDE

mindfulexperience.org

Information on the scientific study of mindfulness, with links to papers reviewing the evidence.

MINDFULNESS RETREATS

mindfulnessretreats.co.uk

For a short break from the city, Ed Halliwell and colleagues run one-day introductions and residential retreats in Sussex, less than one hour's journey from Victoria.

OXFORD MINDFULNESS CENTRE

oxfordmindfulness.org

Downloadable academic papers on the use of mindfulness for working with specific mental health challenges such as bipolar disorder, suicidal behaviour and eating disorders.

INDEX

Central

North

South

INDEX

Published in 2014 by Virgin Books, an imprint of Ebury Publishing
A Random House Group Company

The Random House Group Limited Reg. No. 954009

Addresses for companies within the Random House Group can be found at
www.randomhouse.co.uk

A CIP catalogue record for this book is available from the British Library

The Random House Group Limited supports the Forest Stewardship Council® (FSC®),
the leading international forest-certification organisation. Our books carrying the FSC
label are printed on FSC®-certified paper. FSC is the only forest-certification scheme
supported by the leading environmental organisations, including Greenpeace. Our
paper procurement policy can be found at www.randomhouse.co.uk/environment

MIX
Paper from
responsible sources
FSC® C011124

Printed and bound in Germany by Mohn Media GmbH

ISBN 9780753555699

To buy books by your favourite authors and register for offers visit
www.randomhouse.co.uk